OUT IN THE **COLD**

OUT IN THE COLD

EMERGENCY WATER SUPPLY AND SANITATION FOR COLD REGIONS

Mark Buttle and Michael Smith

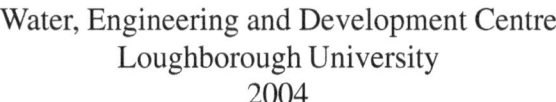

Water, Engineering and Development Centre
Loughborough University
2004

Water, Engineering and Development Centre,
Loughborough University,
Leicestershire, LE11 3TU, UK

© Water, Engineering and Development Centre Loughborough University 2004

ISBN 13 Paperback: 978 1 84380 077 4
ISBN Ebook: 9781788533140
Book DOI: http://dx.doi.org/10.3362/9781788533140

All rights reserved. No part of this publication may be reprinted or reproduced or utilized in any form or by any electronic, mechanical, or other means, now known or hereafter invented, including photocopying and recording, or in any information storage or retrieval system, without the written permission of the publishers.

A catalogue record for this book is available from the British Library.

A reference copy of this publication is also available online at:
http://www.lboro.ac.uk/wedc/publications/

Buttle, M.A. and Smith, M.D. (2004)
Out in the Cold:
Emergency water supply and sanitation for cold regions
WEDC, Loughborough University, UK.

Third edition
First edition printed in 1999

WEDC (The Water, Engineering and Development Centre) at Loughborough University in the UK is one of the world's leading institutions concerned with education, training, research and consultancy for the planning, provision and management of physical infrastructure for development in low- and middleincome countries.

This edition is reprinted and distributed by Practical Action Publishing.
Since 1974, Practical Action Publishing has published and disseminated books and information in support of international development work throughout the world. Practical Action Publishing trades only in support of its parent charity objectives and any profits are covenanted back to Practical Action (Charity Reg. No. 247257, Group VAT Registration No. 880 9924 76).

All reasonable precautions have been taken by the WEDC, Loughborough University to verify the information contained in this publication. However, WEDC, Loughborough University does not necessarily endorse the technologies presented in this document. The published material is being distributed without warranty of any kind, either expressed or implied. The responsibility for the interpretation and use of the material lies with the reader. In no event shall the WEDC, Loughborough University be liable for damages as a result of their use.

Illustrations: Ken Chatterton and Rod Shaw
Designed and produced by WEDC Publications

About the authors

Mark Buttle is an independent aid and development consultant specializing in water supply and sanitation issues. Since graduation from Cambridge University in 1992 he has spent much time working abroad, most recently helping to implement sustainable water supply and sanitation projects for Oxfam (GB) in Albania. Also gaining an MSc at WEDC, he is committed to international development work, combining fieldwork with research into water and sanitation issues. His specializations include post-emergency development and the combination of the social and technical aspects of project design and implementation.

Michael Smith is the WEDC MSc Programme Director and a Chartered Civil and Structural Engineer with wide experience of engineering aspects of development projects, including work with refugees. As well as teaching and training, his interests are in the fields of rural water supply, wastewater treatment, sanitation and beneficial re-use of wastewater. His overseas experience includes fieldwork and consultancy work in Lesotho, Sudan, Chad, Honduras, the Palestinian territories, India, China, Peru and Nepal; and training of fieldworkers and technical staff in Bangladesh, Sri Lanka, India, Tanzania and South Africa. Most recently he has experience from China, the Palestinian territories, South Africa and India.

Mark Buttle

Michael Smith

Acknowledgements

The authors would like to thank the following people and organizations:

The Department for International Development (DFID), UK for funding the publication of the first edition of this book.

RedR – Engineers for Disaster Relief and Oxfam (GB), whose members and personnel contributed material for both the original research and this second edition.

Peer reviewers of the original text: Woldu Mahary, Daniel Mora Castro, Murray Biedler, Alain Oppliger, Bob Reed, Sarah House and Sohrab Baghri.

For Heather, from Mark
and
For Isabel from Mike

The views expressed in this book are solely those of the authors and are not representative of the views of organizations that helped in its production. While every effort has been made to ensure that the recommendations made in this manual are correct, the authors would welcome additional suggestions and comments arising from users' experiences in the field.

Contents

Chapter 1: Introduction — 1
1.1 Who this book is aimed at — 1
1.2 How to use *Out in the Cold* — 1
1.3 Scope — 1
1.4 Emergency engineering manuals — 2

Chapter 2: Emergencies in cold regions — 3
2.1 Climatic data — 3
2.2 Emergency environments — 4
 Cold regions — 4
 Urban and rural locations — 4
 Mountain locations and climate — 5
2.3 Winterisation studies — 5
2.4 Appropriate technology for cold regions — 6
 Water supply technology — 6
 Environmental sanitation technology — 7

Chapter 3: Water supply — 8
3.1 Properties of water, ice and snow — 8
 Water density — 8
 Water viscosity — 9
 Ice formation — 9
 Snow — 9
3.2 Sources — 9
 Groundwater — 10
 Surface water — 14
 Purification of lakes or ponds by brine pumping — 17
 Snow — 19
 Hauled water — 21
3.3 Water storage — 21
 Tanks — 21
 Ground storage lakes — 24
3.4 Water treatment — 25
 Mixing and pumping requirements — 25
 Sedimentation tanks — 26
 Chemical disinfection — 26
 Filtration — 26
 Boiling water — 28
 Heating water for washing — 29

3.5	Distribution systems	30
	Leaks	*30*
	Preventing pipes freezing	*30*
	Pipe materials	*33*
	Defrosting pipes blocked by ice	*35*
	Plumbing of hospitals and collective centres	*37*
	Protecting distribution points	*38*
3.6	Water supply in mountainous regions	39
	Water sources and treatment	*39*
	Pressure problems in pipes	*42*
	Pumping at altitude	*42*
3.7	Books on water supply	43

Chapter 4: Sanitation — 44

4.1	Excreta disposal	44
	Open defecation	*44*
	Pit latrines	*45*
	Honey-buckets and honey-bags	*47*
	Hand-washing facilities	*47*
4.2	Conventional sewerage systems	48
	Wastewater treatment	*49*
4.3	Solid waste management	53
4.4	Disposal of the dead	53
4.5	Environmental sanitation in mountainous areas	53
	Excreta disposal in mountainous areas	*53*
	Solid waste and mountain camps	*54*
4.6	Books on sanitation	54

Chapter 5: Related technical issues — 55

5.1	Construction	55
	Using concrete in freezing temperatures	*55*
	Building on frozen ground	*57*
	Calculating snow loads	*58*
5.2	Logistics	59
	Water haulage	*59*
	Stockpiling for winter	*59*
	Use of vehicles for personal transport	*59*
	Chemical control of snow and ice on roads	*60*
	Logistics in mountainous regions	*63*
5.3	Mechanics	64
	Vehicles, pumps and generators	*64*

5.4	Shelter	66
	Rehabilitation of urban shelter	*66*
	Tents	*66*

Chapter 6: Human issues — 68
6.1	Health	68
	Air-borne diseases	*68*
	Water-washed diseases	*68*
	Diseases transmitted by vectors	*69*
	Other health problems	*70*
6.2	Socio-political issues	70
6.3	Personal effectiveness	71
6.4	Health and safety	72

Chapter 7: Additional information — 73
7.1	Appendix A – Water supply flowcharts	73
7.2	Appendix B – Thermal properties and density of materials	77
7.3	Appendix C – Surface pipes, preventing freezing 64	79
7.4	Appendix D – Addresses	83
7.5	References and bibliography	85

Index — 88

List of figures

Figure 3.1.	The effect of a shifting river, in a permafrost area, on groundwater depth and on the location of boreholes	11
Figure 3.2.	Handpumps with features to prevent freezing	13
Figure 3.3.	Seasonal quality variation of water in lakes and quality improvement by brine pumping	16
Figure 3.4.	Temporary water intakes showing arrangements for summer and winter pumping	18
Figure 3.5.	Possible arrangements of infiltration galleries and collector wells	20
Figure 3.6.	Temporary storage tank, showing design features appropriate for cold regions	22
Figure 3.7.	Graph of correction factors for the effect of temperature on viscosity-dominated processes	25
Figure 3.8.	Put and take water heater	29
Figure 3.9.	Recirculating pumped system	32
Figure 3.10.	Plumbing a large building into an intermittent supply	38
Figure 3.11.	Tap box protection of a temporary standpipe	40
Figure 3.12.	Sample design for a break-pressure tank	41
Figure 3.13.	The effect of altitude on available suction head for suction pumps	43
Figure 4.1.	Additional support for latrine slabs	46
Figure 4.2.	A hand-washing facility, showing the insulated bucket (fitted with a tap), basin, soap dish and concrete slab	48
Figure 4.3.	Flow of wastewater through a conventional treatment works	50
Figure 4.4.	Raised mound system for disposal of treated wastewater	52
Figure 6.1.	Graph showing apparent temperature variation with wind speed, known as the wind-chill effect	71
Figure 7.1.	Flowchart for water source selection in cold regions	74
Figure 7.2.	Flowchart for water source selection in mountainous areas	75
Figure 7.3.	Flowchart for assessing the suitability of water sources for survival supply in cold regions	76

List of tables

Table 3.1.	The effect of altitude on the boiling point of water	28
Table 3.2.	Thermal properties of HDPE pipe, bare and insulated	34
Table 3.3.	Approximate current and time for thawing steel pipe	36
Table 3.4.	Recommended cable sizes	36
Table 5.1.	Amount of antifreeze admix added to concrete, by percentage of dry weight	57
Table 5.2.	Advantages and disadvantages of chemicals and abrasives	61
Table 5.3.	Recommended applications of chemicals to paved roads with an average daily traffic of 500 vehicles or more	62
Table 5.4.	Requirements of horses, donkeys and pack ponies	64
Table 5.5.	Mechanical problems with engines	65
Table 7.1.	Thermal properties and density of construction materials	77
Table 7.2.	Thermal properties and density of materials found in the environment	78
Table 7.3.	Design times t_d for water to cool to 0°C from different starting temperatures, for surface laid pipes	80
Table 7.4.	Manufacturers and suppliers	83
Table 7.5.	Agencies and organisations	84

'Out in the cold'

Chapter 1

Introduction

In the 1990s events in Bosnia, the former Soviet Union countries, Afghanistan and Northern Iraq showed that humanitarian disasters are not limited to the South, Africa, or the tropics, but may strike anywhere in the world. Relief workers have had to be ever more adaptable in order to provide life-saving water supplies and sanitation facilities in areas where freezing conditions occur. This second edition of *Out in the Cold* includes new material gathered from humanitarian workers returning from the Kosovo crisis and has been revised on the basis of comments made about the first edition.

1.1 Who this book is aimed at

All humanitarian workers, especially managers, engineers and logisticians working in ex-Soviet states, China, Eastern Europe or any other country in cool temperate or cold regions will find sections of this book relevant to them. Techniques are described fairly simply, although engineering design recommendations are also included.

1.2 How to use *Out in the Cold*

This guide is written in such a way that readers can dip into specific subjects by using the contents and index pages. Basic information is not covered extensively because *Out in the Cold* is designed to provide supplementary information that can be used in addition to the information given in more general emergency manuals, such as those listed on overleaf. This is a specialist guide to cold regions and will not duplicate information already well covered by existing manuals.

1.3 Scope

Out in the Cold takes into account that areas can be cold either because of their geographical location (high latitude, or non-tropical continental interior), or because an area is mountainous and at a relatively higher altitude than the surrounding area. Specific points relating to mountainous areas are incorporated in the text.

Water supply and sanitation (watsan) techniques appropriate for emergencies in warm regions are well documented. Excellent manuals exist, for example *Engineering in Emergencies* by Jan Davis and Bobby Lambert (1995), which describes many techniques that could be used successfully anywhere in the world. However, there are some techniques that are not covered in the emergency manuals because the tendency has been to concentrate on water supply and sanitation systems that are appropriate for use in Africa, South Asia and other warm places.

Engineering techniques introduced in this manual are specifically designed to be used for emergencies in areas where freezing conditions are likely to cause problems, although wider issues relating to the provision of water supply and sanitation in all cold areas are also discussed. The fact that techniques appropriate in cold regions are different affects the planning and location of refugee camps (needs assessments), the sourcing of appropriate materials (logistics) and the associated management of emergency operations.

1.4 Emergency engineering manuals

The following provide technical advice for use in emergency situations, although they do not specifically address cold climate emergency considerations:

1. Assar, M, 1971, *Guide to Sanitation in Natural Disasters*. WHO, Geneva, Switzerland
2. Davis, Jan and Lambert, Robert, 1995, *Engineering in Emergencies, A Practical Guide for Relief Workers*. IT Publications, London, UK
3. House, Sarah and Reed, Bob, 1997, *Emergency Water Sources, Guidelines for Selection and Treatment*. WEDC, Loughborough, UK
4. MSF, 1994, *Public Health Engineering in Emergency Situations*. MSF, Paris, France
5. Ockwell, Ron, 1986, *Assisting in Emergencies, A Resource Handbook for UNICEF Field Staff*. UNICEF, Geneva, Switzerland
6. UNHCR, 1982, *Handbook for Emergencies, Part One, Field Operations*. UNHCR, Geneva, Switzerland
7. UNHCR, 1992, *Water Manual for Refugee Situations*. UNHCR, Programme and Technical Support Section, Geneva, Switzerland

An additional bibliography, including books about utilities engineering in cold regions and emergency water and sanitation, can be found in section 7.5.

Chapter 2

Emergencies in cold regions

2.1 Climatic data

Winter freeze-ups affect water supply and sanitation options, logistics, construction techniques and the health of the population. Even people's attitudes to work are adversely affected by the cold. To increase the effectiveness of aid provision, therefore, it is essential to obtain reliable climatic data. Basic climate information should include answers to the following questions:

About the winter
- When does the winter period start and finish?
- Are temperatures below freezing at night only or also during the day?
- What are the average daytime and night-time temperatures in winter?
- What is the minimum temperature likely to be?
- How much snow can be expected and at what time of year?

About the summer
- When does the summer period start and finish?
- Is there a period when there will not be a frost, even at night?
- What are the average day-time and night-time summer temperatures?

Also
- How much precipitation falls as rain? When?
- How many hours of daylight and darkness are there in the summer and how many in the winter?

Apart from talking to local people, climatic information is available from local meteorological stations (at airports or military establishments), media companies (TV, radio or newspaper), or on the Internet.

Monthly temperature and precipitation data for many cities around the world are given in *The World Weather Guide*.[1]

---

[1] Pearce and Smith (1998)

2.2 Emergency environments

It is worth considering how the winterised emergency differs from those that happen in warmer areas. Not only are the required technologies and approaches different, but also people living in one environment find it difficult to move to another. This was true of the Kurds who fled into the mountains of Northern Iraq in 1991, and who then suffered greatly, partly because they were used to living lower down on the plains.

Cold regions

If the definition of a cold region is taken to be an area where the average (mean) temperature is below 1°C for more than one month of each year, then over 1 billion people live in such an area.[2] For the purposes of this book 'cold regions' include anywhere where the temperature is likely to fall below 0°C for long enough to have an adverse effect on water supply or sanitation.

Urban and rural locations

Appropriate emergency watsan interventions vary, of course, depending on whether the affected population is in a rural or urban location, for example, or whether they are living in a temporary camp or mainly in houses as most Kosovar refugees did in Albania in 1999. The main differences between the urban and rural cases will be differences in the levels of technology used, although other factors include the more variable standard of education and the effects of seasonal work on community participation in rural areas.

In an urban setting repairing existing water supply and sewerage networks is the main priority in order to minimise further deterioration. These systems require the knowledge of experienced engineers. By repairing such systems large numbers of people quickly receive the benefits of clean water and sanitary conditions, reducing the associated health risks. As a guide only, some measures appropriate for the renovation of an urban sewerage system are included in Chapter 4. Methods of plumbing in collective centres and hospitals are discussed in Chapter 3.

In urban areas, aid agencies often find themselves repairing local facilities: fixing doors, windows, floors, and so on. Local people are often unable to obtain construction materials for financial, logistical or political reasons.[3]

In rural locations, or camps, the emphasis of watsan provision is on the development of new sources of water, and setting up new sanitation systems. However, in many countries even small villages are likely to have systems that could, and should, be renovated if at all possible.

Levels of development in different regions of the same country, or in different countries are often highly variable. This is even more confusing in countries in colder regions, many of which were highly developed prior to any disaster. For example, cities in the former Soviet Union countries or eastern Europe have almost certainly had working water supply, sewer-

---

[2] Smith (1996)
[3] Buttle (1998)

age, gas and electricity systems in the past, but in some of these areas regional disaster has greatly reduced the local level of development. Many rural and urban areas within the former Soviet Union countries, central Asia or eastern Europe could now be considered as underdeveloped, regardless of their previous level of development.

Mountain locations and climate

In addition to areas where the predominant climate is cool temperate or cold, cold regions must also include mountainous areas. Altitude causes a reduction in the ambient temperature. A fall in temperature of between 1.5°C (in moist air) and 3°C (in very dry air) should be expected for every 300m of altitude gained.[4] In addition, mountainous areas are often very exposed, so people forced to move through or live in those areas also suffer because of the rapid loss of body heat due to the cooling effect of winds. The wind-chill effect causes the apparent temperature to be less than the true temperature.

The ability of a displaced population to survive in the mountains is greatly hindered if they are not used to living in such conditions. This happened in Northern Iraq after the Gulf War in 1991, when some Kurdish refugees originated from mountainous areas, but many others had fled to the mountains from much warmer areas, and suffered greatly as a result.

In the mountains the positioning of water supply distribution points, latrines and any other facilities must take into account not only their location, but the location of areas where people will have to queue. This is partly to minimise the time people take to walk to the facilities in the cold, but also to take care that people are not forced to cross steep or loose areas of mountainside to get there. Areas for distribution should also be organised carefully to minimise the risks from exposure and physical harm.

2.3   Winterisation studies

At the start of any emergency, a rapid assessment of the situation is made, leading to a plan of action. Planning for the next season is an important activity throughout the year. In cold regions this planning aspect needs to be repeated annually in preparation for each oncoming winter.

Winterisation studies should be done in the summer, to allow sufficient time to implement measures necessary to prepare for winter. The aims of such studies are, firstly, to predict the factors that will (or could) affect the provision of aid during the winter period and, secondly, to determine what can be done by way of preparation to overcome the difficulties.

Likely issues include:

Shelter
- Are the current shelter options going to beadequate in winter, or not?
- What general shelter improvements can be made – provision, upgrading and repairs?
- How well is the area drained? What will happen to the groundwater level?
- How will heating be provided?

---

[4] Walker (1988)

Water supply and sanitation (watsan)
- Which systems are at risk of freezing, what damage will result if they do freeze, and what can be done to protect those systems? To what depth will the ground freeze?
- Are there social reasons for changing water supply or sanitation practices in the winter (e.g. toilets are too cold or too far away from accomodation and people will not use them; washing water needs heating)?
- Is it possible to construct new facilities in winter? By what date should projects be completed?
- How will the cold affect the maintenance of watsan facilities (e.g. more work may be necessary to drain distribution pipes; cold weather may make workers less inclined to work)?
- Is it possible to collect solid waste from all areas in winter?

Logistics
- What areas are likely to be completely cut off by the weather, and what areas are likely to be difficult to reach?
- Which items should be stockpiled, (e.g. food, fuel, blankets, warm clothing, shelter materials, or bags to contain wastes)? Is extra warehousing necessary, and is it possible to provide it?
- How will winter weather (e.g. snow or icy roads) affect access to disaster-affected areas, and what effect will any lack of access have on current systems, such as hauled water?

Physical threats
- What risks of flooding exist, including from snowmelt in the spring?
- Is there a risk from landslides or avalanches?

Human issues
- How will adverse weather affect local people's attitudes? For example people may show less motivation to work in cold weather, or may become so preoccupied with money, food, shelter and warmth that water supply and sanitation become a very low priority.
- What winter-related health problems are likely (e.g. respiratory diseases)?
- What can be done to minimise these health problems?
- What can be done to help the most vulnerable members of the community, such as older people and young children?

2.4 Appropriate technology for cold regions

Water supply technology
Equipment from donor agencies, although well tried and tested in Africa, is not always suitable for use in colder countries. Oxfam storage tanks, for example, have had problems with both water freezing over (tank liners could easily be damaged by ice forming on the water's surface) and roofs collapsing under a snow load. Problems have been overcome, in some instances, by erecting the tanks indoors. The other main difficulties arise when distribution networks freeze: ice forming in pipes and valves is liable to damage them.

The technology used for an emergency water supply in the tropics is not always suitable for the winter in central Asia, in which case it is necessary to use technology and techniques that are specifically designed for use in cold regions. Examples of the use of effective technology include insulating water tanks, burying pipes, and designing water treatment processes that take into account slower rates of reactions and the higher viscosity of water at lower temperatures. Water supply matters are discussed in more detail in Chapter 3.

Environmental sanitation technology

As in warmer climates, sanitation options always need to be considered in the context of cultural and religious acceptability, however cooler temperatures do affect the range of technologies that it is possible to use. The actions of pit latrines and septic tanks are impeded by cold temperatures. However technology that is used in everyday life in, for example, Alaska can be successfully adapted for use in humanitarian aid programmes following disasters in cold regions.

The rates of biological reactions, which are critical to the decomposition processes that are used to treat excreta and wastewater, are greatly reduced at low temperatures. In some areas excreta has to be stored throughout the winter, until ambient temperatures are sufficient for treatment processes. In other cases, emptying on-site excreta disposal facilities more frequently and more reliably than in warm climates can solve the problem. Excreta disposal technology and other sanitation issues are discussed more thoroughly in Chapter 4.

Chapter 3

Water supply

Although the subject of water supply is well covered in many emergency manuals, there are additional factors which will affect the provision of fresh water for domestic supplies in conditions where the ambient temperature is close to or below 0°C. Chemical reactions are slower at low temperatures and biological processes also take more time. The physical properties of water, in the form of water, ice or snow, are temperature dependent, therefore affect processes involved in supplying water and the range of technology that can be used.

The provision of water supply and sanitation is always closely related to the type of shelter in which the affected population is living. This is more so in cold regions where the provision of shelter is obviously a high priority. Specific shelter options are discussed at greater length in Section 5.4.

3.1 Properties of water, ice and snow

Water density

As liquid water cools its density gradually increases, a behaviour that is typical of most liquids. However water reaches its maximum density at 4°C, below which the density decreases slightly: the water expands, until ice begins to form at 0°C. As it congeals into ice it gains approximately 9% of its liquid volume, consequently ice is less dense than water, and floats.[5]

The fact that water is most dense at 4°C causes a quality fluctuation in the water in lakes in cold regions. During the autumn, as the water slowly cools, the warmer and colder layers 'turn over' causing a sudden, temporary, increase in Total Dissolved Solids (TDS).[6] Sediments, containing suspended solids and soluble materials, will be disturbed as the warmer and colder water layers mix. As the temperature of the top layer of water falls below 4°C, it sinks and disturbs water at greater depth. Also, in winter the warmest water in lakes is at the bottom, whereas it is at the surface during the summertime.

---

[5] Davis and Day (1964)
[6] Smith (1996)

Water viscosity

As water temperature decreases, its viscosity increases. This increase in viscosity reduces the settling velocity of suspended particles (affecting the design of sedimentation tanks) as well as increasing the energy requirements for mixing and pumping operations.

Ice formation

When water freezes and becomes ice the effect of its expansion can exert pressures as high as 2500kg/cm^2. To put this into perspective, it is the same as a static head of water approximately 25km high. These high pressures inevitably cause problems if water freezes in pipes, pumps or other containers which cannot withstand such large forces.

Snow

Properties of snow vary greatly according to how old it is. New snow is less dense than old, more compacted snow, and has better insulating properties. Surprisingly, perhaps, all snow is a relatively good insulator: its thermal conductivity, even when dense, is much less than that of ice. This affects not only how much heat is lost from buildings, but also the rate of formation of lake and river ice.[7] In Canada and Alaska, settlers used to pile snow against their wooden buildings in order to increase the insulating properties of the walls.

A snow covering of 1 to 10cm in depth raises the temperature of the surface of the ground by 1.1°C above air temperature for each centimetre of snow depth (although the ground temperature cannot be greater than 0°C). Even at pipe-burial depths (e.g. 0.6m to 2m) a covering of snow will raise the temperature of the soil by at least 0.1°C per cm of snow cover, compared to the temperature at the same depth of uncovered or cleared ground.[8]

3.2 Sources

If there is no 'urban' water supply, or if it is temporarily unusable, water source options for abstracting water for drinking, cooking and washing obviously depend on what sources exist in the local area. Snow or other winter weather which makes trucked water deliveries impossible may also mean that the development of local water sources is a priority.

Appendix A contains flowcharts that can be used to aid the selection of appropriate water sources for emergency use in cold regions. Whilst these flowcharts concentrate on technical issues, it must be stressed that social, religious, environmental, and financial (cost) implications are also important factors to be considered when selecting appropriate water sources. *Emergency Water Sources* offers a comprehensive description of many issues connected with this subject.[9] This section describes some of the factors that will affect the choice of supply in a cold region, and which are additional to the normal factors of proximity, water quality, adequate volume and cost that will always affect source selection decisions.

---

[7] Langham (1981)
[8] Steppuhn (1981)
[9] House and Reed (1997)

Groundwater

Being warmer than surface water, and with temperatures and quality that are generally constant throughout the year, groundwater offers several advantages over surface water as a potential water source in cold regions.

These advantages include:
- The higher temperature of groundwater makes it less likely that water will freeze in storage tanks or distribution pipes.
- The reliability of temperature and quality means that the same water treatment regime can be used all year round. Seasonal quality and temperature variations of surface water sources can make its treatment options more complicated.

One potential problem associated with using groundwater is that above-ground pumps are liable to maintenance problems or damage from frost, although submerged ones will be protected (insulated) by the water. (See section 5.3 *Mechanics*.)

Positive and negative factors should also be weighed up against factors that are common to warm or cold climates, such as:
- Properly protected wells and boreholes can have extremely low levels of faecal pollution, minimising health risks and treatment costs.
- Water quality varies depending on local hydrogeological conditions. The water may have a high mineral content, including dissolved metals and salts, which could make the water unpotable, or minerals such as arsenic and fluoride which have associated health problems. In any case, a full physical and chemical analysis of the water should always be carried out.
- Location and development of groundwater sources can be very expensive.

Wells and boreholes

When constructing wells and boreholes in areas where the ground is liable to freeze, bentonite (clay) should be used, instead of concrete, for grouting the annular space around the casing (to prevent the flow of surface water, containing pollutants, into the hole). Concrete can bond tightly to steel well casings, whereupon frost heave, caused by the annual freezing of the ground, then pulls the casing apart, ruining the well or borehole.[10]

In permafrost areas, the frozen ground acts as an impermeable layer above groundwater aquifers. Surface water features such as rivers and lakes cause the permanently frozen ground to thaw below them, so that it is possible to locate groundwater closer to the surface near to surface water features. Figure 3.1 shows how boreholes located on the inside of river bends can access groundwater at a depth where the ground of the surrounding area is permanently frozen.

Springs

It is easy to assume that the water inside a spring box is unlikely to freeze, because the water is continually flowing and because the water, having originated underground, would nor-

---
[10] Smith (1996)

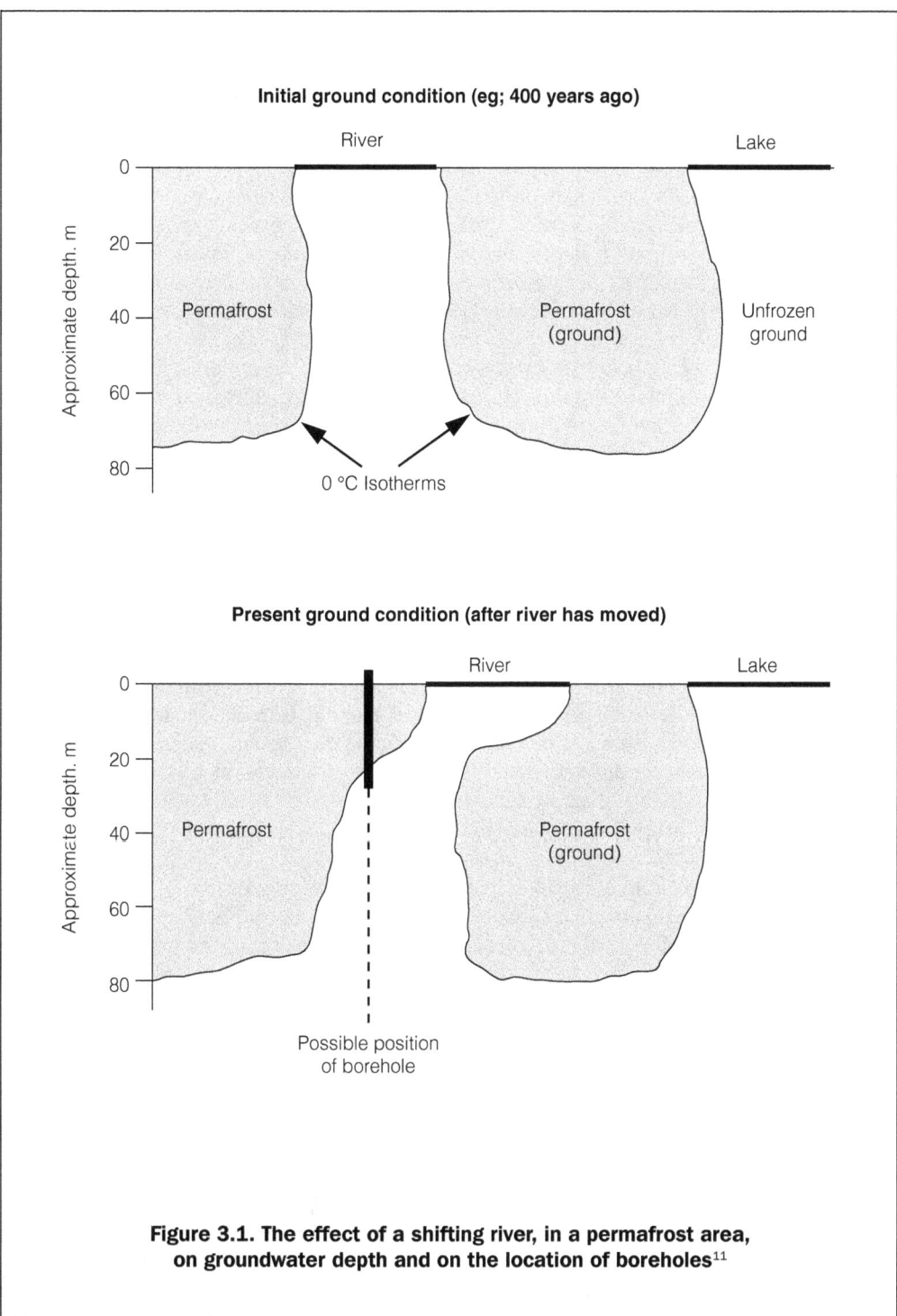

Figure 3.1. The effect of a shifting river, in a permafrost area, on groundwater depth and on the location of boreholes[11]

---

[11] adapted from Smith (1996)

mally be slightly warmer than surface water. However in mountainous areas freeze-ups and other problems are possible.

First, in mountainous areas, water emerging from springs is likely to be quite cold already, having originated higher up the slope. This increases the likelihood of the water freezing during a cold spell. If outlets from a spring box do freeze up, the resulting back-pressure may cause subterranean water flow channels to alter their course, causing the spring to emerge at a different place! It is essential to guard against freeze-ups by covering spring boxes with an insulating layer of soil, of a depth equivalent to the depth of maximum winter frost penetration in the ground, so that water in the spring box is never cooled to below 0°C. A thickness of 0.75m to 1m of soil cover provides adequate insulation for most situations.

Secondly, building spring boxes in scree is very likely to cause problems. In scree subterranean flows can alter course periodically, causing the spring to emerge at a different place. The spring protection then has to be moved to the new location where the water emerges from the ground, or new protection facilities built. Scree movements are also likely to damage spring boxes, necessitating continual maintenance. If it is impossible to avoid scree, use local materials, as it is very likely that the spring box will have to be replaced periodically.

Handpumps

Soil will provide some thermal insulation, so underground water may remain unfrozen even when air temperatures above ground are below freezing. Whether groundwater freezes or not depends on the depth to the groundwater, the air temperature and the insulating properties of materials separating the water from the air above ground. In addition, groundwater will freeze from the top down, so water below the water table may remain unfrozen even if water close to the top of the water table freezes. Whatever type of handpump is used, some damage due to freezing is possible. Features useful for all types of handpump installed where temperatures can fall below freezing include:

- Locate pumps in a pump house to help prevent water freezing inside.
- Ice is likely to form on concrete aprons around boreholes and wells. Care should be taken to provide good drainage, and to encourage people not to splash water around if at all possible.
- Allow water in the riser pipe to drain down to groundwater level when the pump is not being used, to reduce the likelihood of water freezing. Figure 3.2 shows four different types of hand pump, with small dots indicating possible places where holes could be made in the riser pipe to allow water to drain when the pump is not in use without seriously affecting the performance of the pump.

Lift pumps

These are distinguished from suction pumps by the location of the pumping cylinder, which is submerged below the water level in the borehole. Lift pumps are normally used when the dynamic water level is more than 7-8m below ground, making suction impossible. Lift pumps make sense in cold areas precisely because the working parts of the cylinder will always be underground, where they will be insulated from the cold.

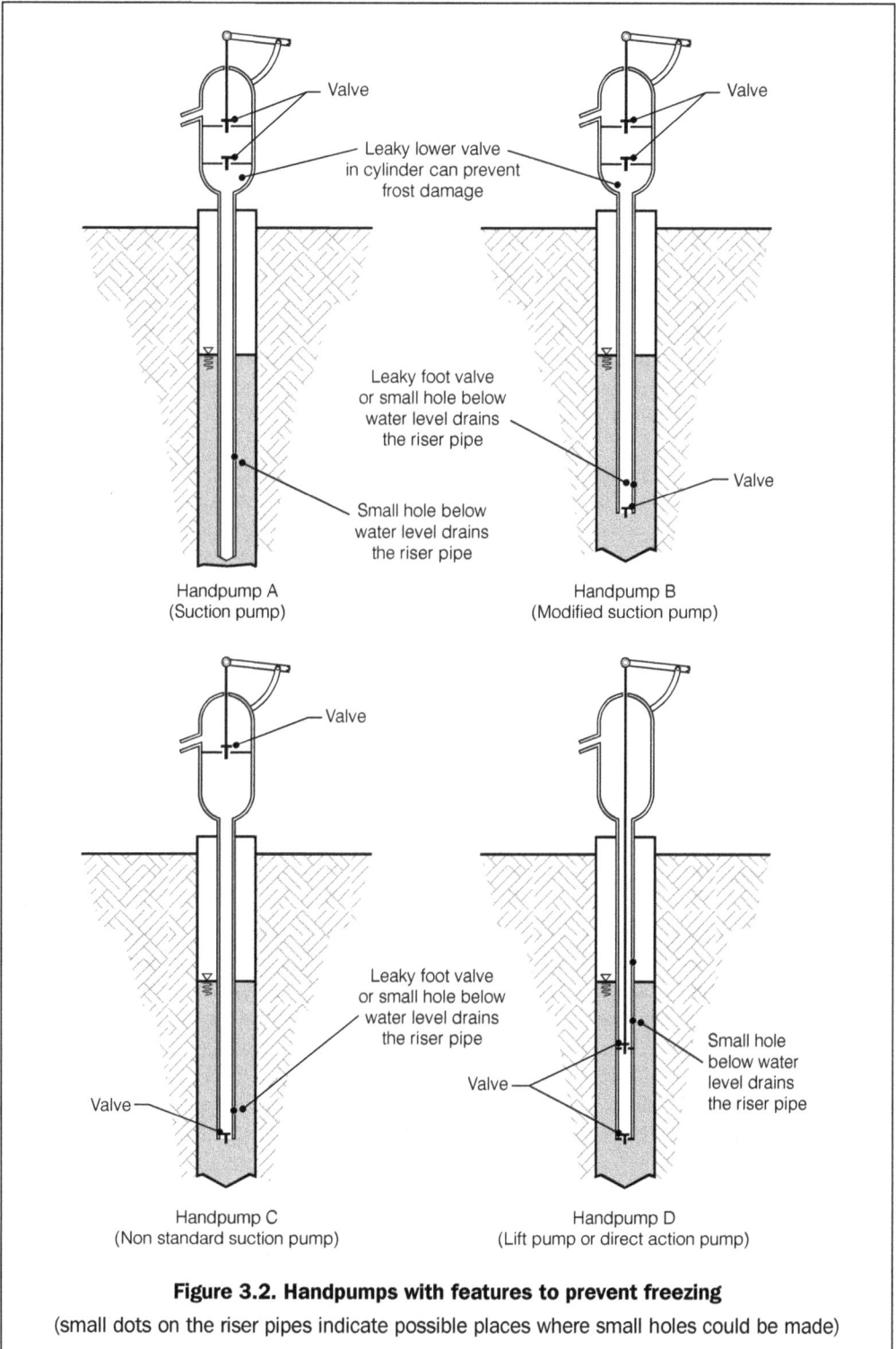

Figure 3.2. Handpumps with features to prevent freezing
(small dots on the riser pipes indicate possible places where small holes could be made)

Above-ground pump parts can be protected by making a small diameter 'weephole' in the riser pipe just above the cylinder (either below groundwater level or above the water table at a depth where freezing will not occur, as shown for Handpump D in Figure 3.2). Water slowly drains out of the above-ground section when the pump is not being used, reducing the likelihood of water freezing in the above- ground pump sections. This causes a small loss in the pumping efficiency, although being below water level the cylinder needs no priming.

Suction pumps
Because the pumping cylinder is above ground, it is prone to damage when the water remaining inside the pump freezes after pumping ceases. One way to protect it is to use a lower valve (in the cylinder) that leaks slightly into the rising main. That way the cylinder drains when the pump is not in use. If there is, instead, a foot valve at the bottom of the riser pipe (a one-way valve), either it can be made to leak slightly, or a small hole can be drilled in the riser pipe just above the foot valve. Note that such a hole must be below the water level or the pump will not function at all (see Figure 3.2, Handpumps A, B, C).

The above measures for suction pumps imply that the pumps will, automatically and slowly, drain themselves of water. There is a loss of pumping efficiency since the water has to be pumped again, and this, obviously, should be minimised. The self-draining nature of the above-ground pump parts may also make it necessary to have water available, close to the pump, for priming the pump. In this case the water needs to be kept indoors, but close to the pumping area, to prevent it freezing at night. Also, it is important that the priming water is kept in a sealed container and protected from pathogenic organisms, which would lead to contamination of the pump and possibly the borehole itself.

Surface water

Quality
Surface water is always liable to be contaminated by faecal pollution, particularly during a disaster, when normal excreta disposal facilities may not be functioning properly. However, incorrect assumptions are often made about the quality of surface water in cold regions.

One myth is that bacteria cannot survive in very cold water. This is not true; bacteria actually survive longer in cold water, although their rate of metabolism is greatly reduced. If consumed by humans their rate of metabolism will increase once more, possibly leading to disease. Living coliforms have been detected in military camps in the Arctic that had been abandoned years earlier.[12] The presence of faecal coliforms in water is an indicator that it has recently been polluted with faecal matter, and that dangerous bacteria and other pathogens could also be present. The possibility of faecal organisms surviving a winter in a refugee camp, only to cause health problems by entering the water supply in the summer, should not be discounted.

There are certain bacteria which are adapted to live in colder conditions (psychrophilic bacteria). If present in drinking water, certain of these could cause health problems. Therefore no assumptions should be made about the water quality of mountain streams, and proper water supplies must be established, with frequent and thorough water testing for quality.

---

[12] DiGiovanni et al. (1962)

Rivers and streams

Many cold-region countries have high concentrations of industry and use modern farming methods. In addition to pollution caused by broken sewerage systems, the destruction or running down of industry and farms during a time of disaster makes it highly likely that rivers and lakes will be polluted by chemicals and livestock wastes. Laboratory testing of water samples is the only reliable way to determine pollution levels. If pollution is detected then this will obviously affect the decision whether or not to use rivers and streams as water sources.

In winter the flow volumes in rivers and streams either increase or decrease depending on whether precipitation falls as rain or snow. In the case of an increased winter flow, this reflects the increased winter rainfall, leading to increased turbidity, and the likelihood of various pollutants being washed into the rivers.

If precipitation upstream falls as snow a reduced river flow will be the result. If it is cold enough the snow stays on the ground instead of melting and flowing into water courses. In addition small streams and minor surface flows are liable to freeze solid instead of joining larger water courses. Some small streams are likely to become completely frozen, with no flow. Quality implications include:

- The reduction in flow originating from surface water runoff implies that in winter a greater proportion of river water will originate from groundwater sources such as springs. If the concentration of minerals in the groundwater is higher than that in surface water runoff (and it is likely to be) then the concentration of dissolved minerals in the river will be higher in winter than in summer.
- River water quality deteriorates significantly in the spring because of the seasonal thaw. Ice and snow that accumulated on the surface of the land in winter melts, washing pollutants into the river. The result is a sudden temporary increase in Total Dissolved Solids (TDS) and turbidity.
- Quality monitoring is necessary at all times of the year to ensure that water treatment processes are able to deal with seasonal variations in water quality.

In extreme cases, during the spring large blocks of ice that are released from areas where the river had been frozen over will float downstream. These blocks can wreak havoc if they collide with structures. They are capable of damaging water intake structures and bridges unless very substantial protection structures are built.

Lakes and ponds

As with rivers and streams, the quality of water in lakes and ponds varies seasonally. One cause of these quality variations is the seasonal change of the water temperature:

- In the autumn it is common for the layers of water to invert, disturbing sediments from the bottom of the lake and causing a sudden temporary increase in turbidity and total dissolved solids.
- In winter impurities are slowly rejected from surface ice as it forms, which increases the concentration of suspended and dissolved solids in the water below the ice.

Seasonal variations of water quality are shown more clearly in Figure 3.3.

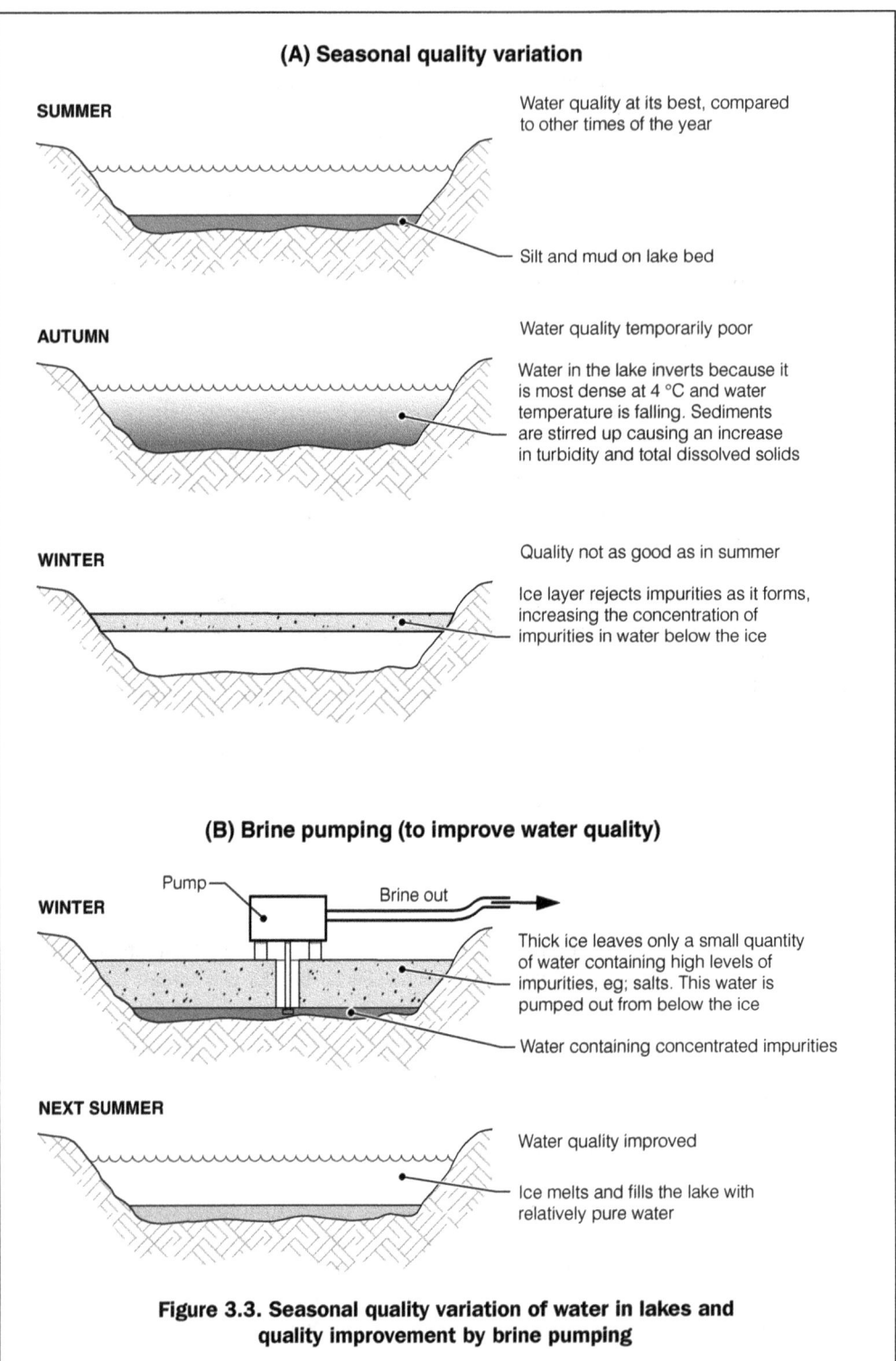

Figure 3.3. Seasonal quality variation of water in lakes and quality improvement by brine pumping

Purification of lakes or ponds by brine pumping

In very cold areas it is possible to purify a shallow lake or pond and prepare it for use as a water source the following year by a process known as brine pumping. Dissolved solids lower the freezing point of water, so ice will only form in solutions at temperatures below 0°C. As the surface of water containing dissolved salts begins to freeze, crystals of pure ice form, and the dissolved salts become concentrated in the remaining solution below and around the ice. As the concentration of salts in the remaining solution increases, the freezing point of the water in the remaining solution is lowered further.

As ice forms on the surface of a lake or pond, impurities are slowly rejected by the freezing water and are therefore concentrated in the remaining water. If most of the water freezes, which is more likely in shallow lakes than in deep ones, then the small amount remaining as a liquid can become highly saline and contain high concentrations of dissolved solids. This water is very unlikely to be suitable for use as a source for domestic supply, however if that liquid portion of the lake water is pumped out and discarded, the majority of soluble pollutants will be removed from the entire lake in one action. When the ice melts in the spring, the water in the lake will contain substantially less Total Dissolved Solids (TDS) than the year before, and may therefore be more suitable as a source of drinking water. Purification of lakes by brine pumping is illustrated in Figure 3.3.

Ice cutting from lakes

Since impurities are rejected from ice forming on the surface of lakes, the ice remains fairly pure. Provided it is handled and stored carefully, cut ice is a valid source of water. Cut ice has been used as a source of water in remote villages in Alaska for many years. Key factors are:

- The fuel and stoves necessary to melt the ice will require some organisation.
- Unless cutting is well organised, people moving around will pollute the frozen lake surface.
- The ice may not be thick enough to support people moving around on it, and falling through could be fatal, so great caution is necessary when investigating this option.

Intakes

Intakes for extracting water from lakes that are liable to freeze over need to incorporate various design features to prevent damage of equipment. To pump from an ice-covered lake or river one temporary solution is to pump intermittently using a portable pump which is located on either the ice or the shore. The pump needs either to be protected from the elements or to be removed in between pumping times. The pipe over the ice should be propped at a continual gradient, using wood blocks, so that water drains back into the lake after the pump has been removed. Possible intake arrangements for winter and summer pumping are shown in Figure 3.4.

Infiltration galleries

In wide gravelly rivers, the winter flow may be under a thick layer of ice and its path through river gravels can shift frequently. Smaller rivers and streams may appear to have frozen completely, but a sub-surface flow may continue throughout the winter. In these conditions water abstraction is difficult: a shifting flow means that it may be difficult to locate running water and the point of abstraction may have to be moved frequently. Utility providers in

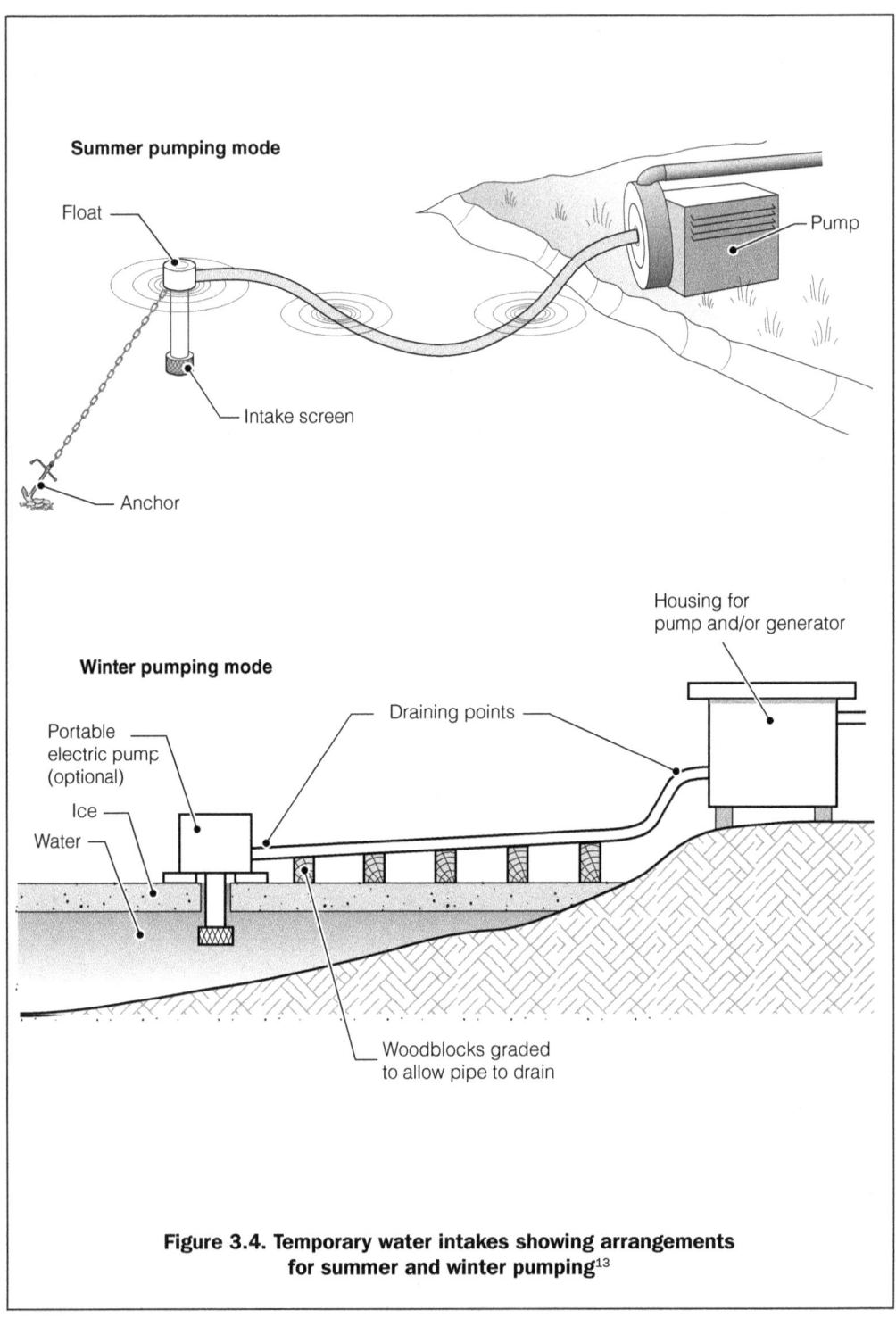

Figure 3.4. Temporary water intakes showing arrangements for summer and winter pumping[13]

---

[13] adapted from Smith (1996)

Alaska overcome these problems by using infiltration galleries that span the width of the riverbed. Infiltration galleries are effective because they avoid the necessity to locate the flow under the ice and, even when surface flow has ceased altogether, a subsurface flow of water may continue.

Generally infiltration galleries are expensive and take considerable effort to construct, and therefore cannot be classified a low technology, emergency solution to water source problems. Repair or renovation requires experienced engineering skill. However it may be viable to construct collector wells with either a horizontal infiltration gallery parallel to the water's edge or with a gravel-filled channel connecting the well to the main body of surface water. Figure 3.5 shows possible arrangements for infiltration galleries and collector wells.

Construction of infiltration galleries requires that:
- the ground in which the gallery is to be placed is not frozen or, in a permafrost area, the ground is in the thaw bulb area where the ground is kept at above 0°C by the heat of the water in the main water body; and
- the ground is permeable. (A coarse-grained medium, such as sand or gravel, is better than a fine-grained one, such as silt.)

Infiltration galleries beside small streams may continue to yield water even when the stream is completely frozen, if there is some subsurface flow.

Snow

For a while snow was the main source of water for Kurdish refugees who were surviving in the mountains of northern Iraq in 1991, and was also used in some rural parts of Bosnia in the wintertime.[14] Therefore it is worth considering snow as a water source even if only as a temporary or seasonal option. Factors include:

- The logistical requirements to distribute materials to melt snow are considerable: cooking vessels, fuel and, possibly, heavy duty plastic bags so that teams can collect large volumes of snow more easily.
- After melting, the water must be treated to kill pathogens. Either the water should be boiled to kill pathogens (an extra fuel requirement, but a convenient option), or small batches should be treated with chlorine tablets (see also the water treatment section, 3.4).

It is also important to note:
- Snow is easily contaminated, therefore it is essential to define and rope off suitable areas/snowfields for use only as a water source.
- Snow should never be eaten, as it greatly lowers the body temperature, causing risk of hypothermia. Snow must be melted before drinking because snow may be much colder than 0°C.
- Potential hazards exist in mountainous areas, such as loose snowfields where there may be a risk from avalanches, or where people collecting snow may be exposed to risk of injury from exposure or falling.

---

[14] Potts (1993)

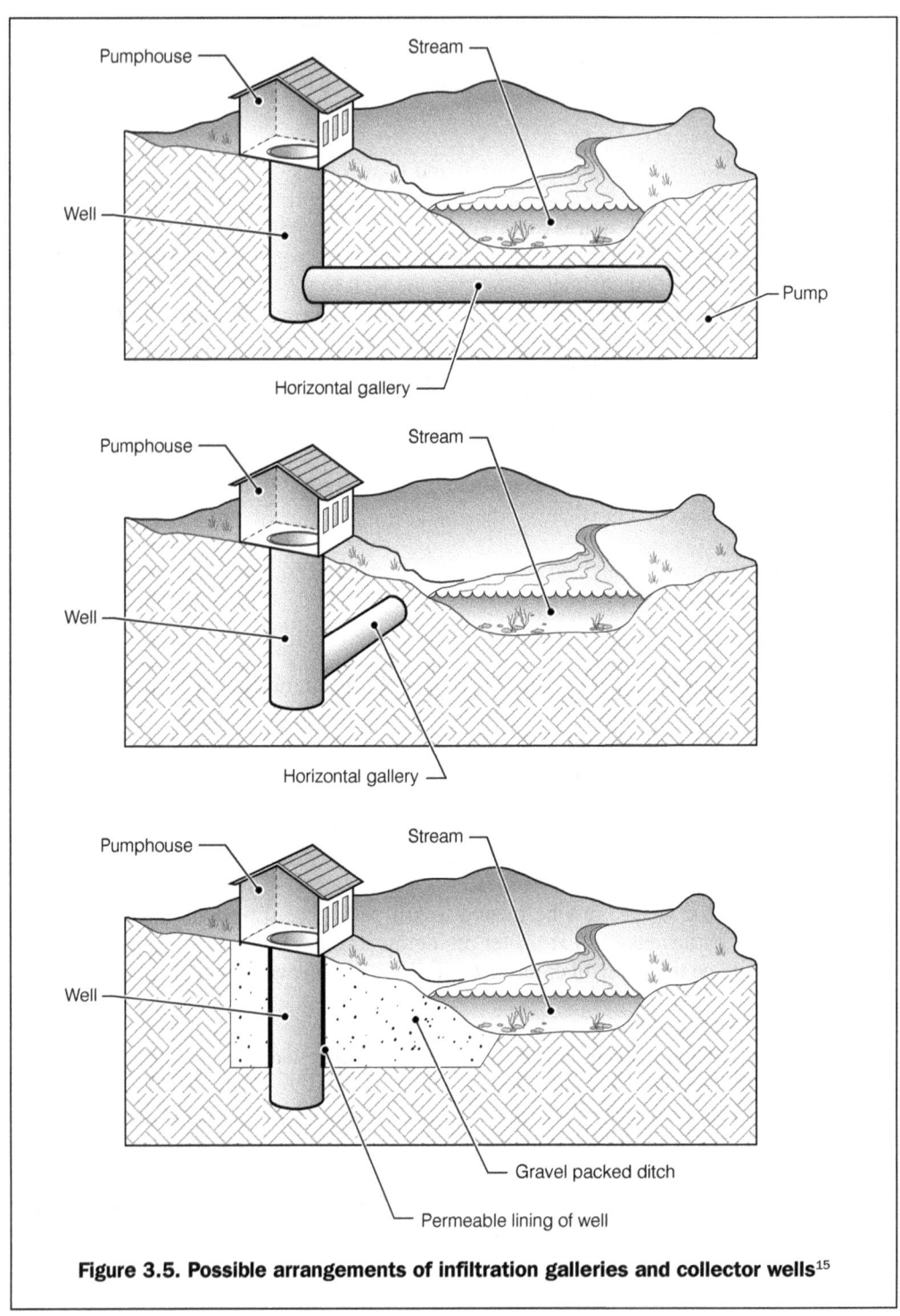

Figure 3.5. Possible arrangements of infiltration galleries and collector wells[15]

---

[15] adapted from Smith (1996)

WATER SUPPLY

- Snow is not very compact. The volume of water collected by melting snow will range from 10% to 40% depending on the age of the snow (old snow is more compact than fresh snow).

Snow has been used as an emergency water source in the past and, as such, should be considered seriously for future use.

Hauled water

The use of tanker trucks and water trailer tanks pulled by tractors to bring water into a disaster area is an established practice where it is difficult or impossible to do anything else. The practice is logistically complicated, very expensive, and other arrangements should be made if at all possible. In cold regions there are some additional factors to consider:

- In winter vehicles may not be able to reach certain areas, especially mountain regions. In these circumstances very local water sources must be used, or the entire population will have to move away from the area.
- Trucks and tractors should be equipped with snow chains and shovels, and should not be forced to make dangerous journeys (e.g. along icy mountain roads) unless it is absolutely unavoidable.
- Maintenance issues are more complicated. Possible difficulties include: diesel gelling, drinking water freezing in tanks and pipes, antifreeze being necessary in coolant water and screenwash, and the need for indoor parking (see also section 5.3).

The logistics and the mechanics sections (5.5 and 5.3) are also relevant to hauled water.

3.3 Water storage

Tanks

Storage tanks donated by international aid organisations have had problems with water freezing inside and causing damage to liners, valves freezing up, and snow breaking flimsy canvas roofs. 'Onion' or 'bladder' tanks are especially unsuitable if there is any risk of water freezing inside them. Short of redesigning or adapting both rigid tanks and bladder tanks, the only way to overcome these problems is to locate the tanks inside heated buildings (e.g. warehouses, other industrial buildings or barns).

Figure 3.6 shows some of the possible features that are useful for temporary storage tanks cold regions.

New tank designs or modifications should take into account the factors below which will help to reduce the probability of the water freezing inside, and minimise damage to the tank if it does so.

Factors that affect all tanks when water freezes inside
- Tank outlet valves should be protected by insulating them. A 'valve-box' lined with insulating foam will help to prevent damage from frost.
- Attachments protruding on the inside of a tank (e.g. ladders) will be ripped off if surface ice forms and then the water level goes up or down. This could rupture the tank walls. Avoid designing any fixtures on the inside of tanks.

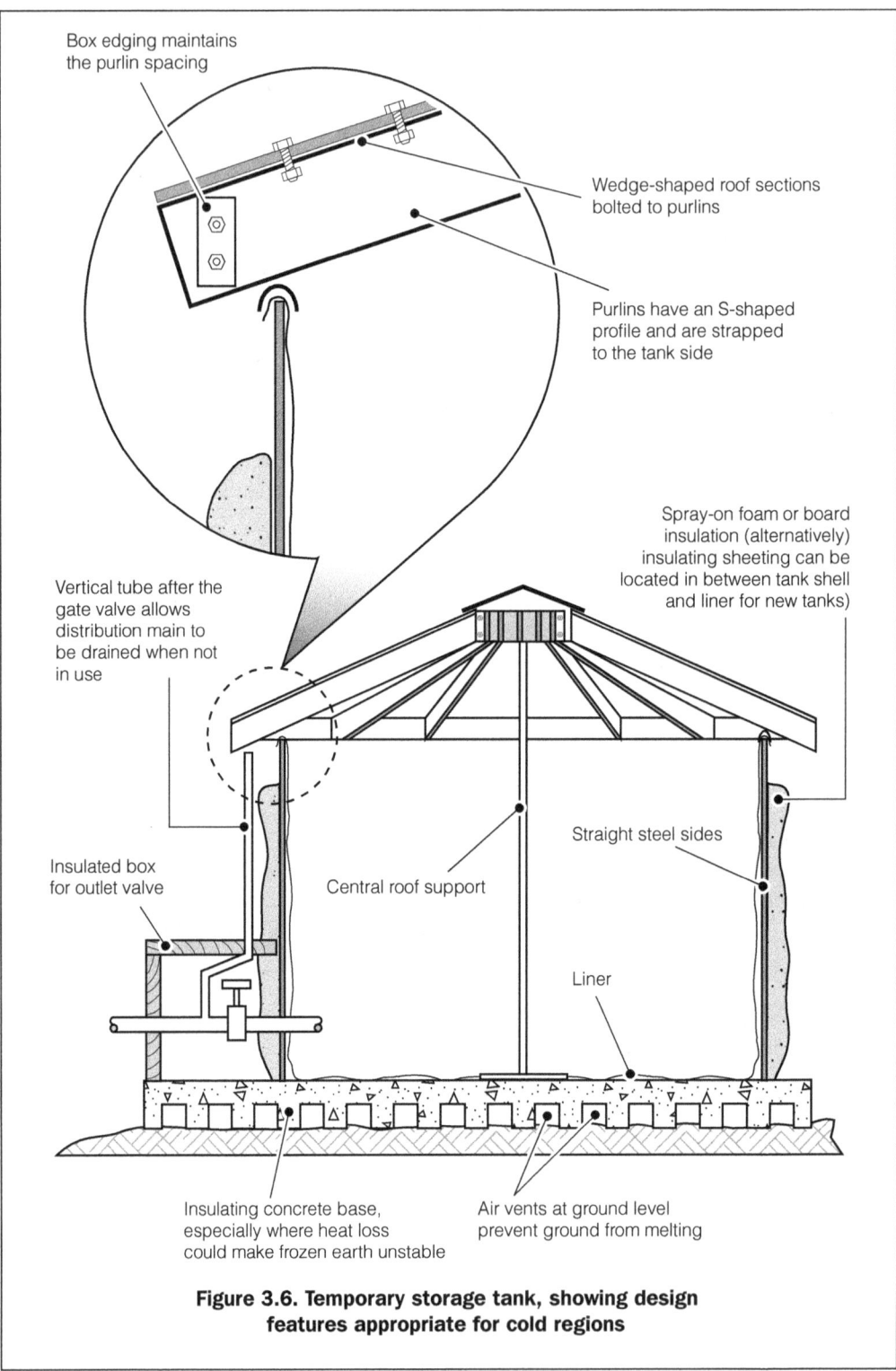

Figure 3.6. Temporary storage tank, showing design features appropriate for cold regions

- If the distribution network needs to be drained at night then a vertical air inlet pipe (higher than the maximum water level in the tank) should be added directly after the gate valve at the tank outlet. This will allow the distribution network to be drained without draining the tank, or subjecting the pipes to negative pressure, which could damage them.
- If there is a continuous flow into the tank (no matter how small) it will help to prevent freezing.
- It has been suggested that some heating of water in tanks would also help to prevent freezing. Raising the water temperature by just one or two degrees could be enough to stop damage due to water freezing. Suggested heating methods include installing a submerged length of high-resistance heating wire (protected from tank liners) connected to a suitable electrical supply; bubbling steam through the water; and heating batches of water separately on a stove. However, the value of using power to do this is debatable, and would need considerable organisation in terms of operation and maintenance.
- Locally made tanks can overcome some of the problems usually associated with outdoor tanks in a cold area, since the local engineers will know designs that are appropriate. In some ex-communist countries the local water authorities have standard designs for water tanks that contractors can build surprisingly quickly.

Insulating existing or new temporary storage tanks
There are several ways to insulate an outside, temporary tank from the surrounding cold air:

- Spray-on polyurethane foam insulation. This minimises the volume of materials to be transported, but application requires dry weather; minimal wind conditions; the tank surface to be dry and clean; surface temperature above 15°C; and air temperature above 10°C.
- Insulating boards can be glued or strapped to the outside of the tank. Boards should be less than 75mm thick to allow installation on curved surfaces. For moist locations a closed cell material that will not absorb water should be used, since wet insulation is much less effective than dry insulation (e.g. closed cell polystyrene or polyurethane). If possible protect boards from getting wet, weathering, birds, and animals by covering them with a cladding material such as plastic sheeting.
- For a new tank, fit insulating boards between the rubber liner and the outer wall of the tank. Boards should be chamfered around outlets, so that the liner fits snugly around flanged fittings.[16]
- Pile earth around the tank. This is a simple and effective solution that also increases tank stability. Wet earth loses its insulating properties, however, and piled-up earth will make the tank roof and inlets accessible to more people, risking roof damage or contamination of the water.
- Tanks can be insulated from the ground by mounting them on insulating concrete or wooden bases. Tanks may be mounted on bases for two reasons:
    1. The water is kept as warm as possible, minimising the risk of it freezing from contact with frozen ground.
    2. If frozen ground is allowed to defrost it can become structurally unstable. Insulating tanks from the ground avoids this problem by reducing the likelihood of the water thawing out the ground. Air vents incorporated in the underside of a concrete base also

---

[16] Gould (2001)

help to maintain the low ground temperature.[17] At the very least a 10cm layer of gravel will help. Meanwhile the concrete base itself helps to spread the load on potentially unstable ground. Aggregates used to make insulating concrete are listed in section 5.1.

- If ground conditions permit, a tank located underground is less likely to freeze due to the insulating effect of the earth surrounding it. Extreme caution should be exercised, however, since the rubber liner of the tank will float if the groundwater level rises above floor level. Do not construct tanks underground if insufficient information about winter groundwater levels is available. In addition, the ground must be stable and able to be excavated, i.e. not already frozen.
- Tank roofs need to be designed to carry snow loads, however the rope and canvas roofs of most temporary tanks will sag and may tear. Snow is actually a good insulator, so avoid brushing it off if you can! Galvanised steel roofs for 'Oxfam' type tanks are available from Evenproducts Ltd in the UK (address and website in section 7.4).

Otherwise a simple roof can be fabricated locally. The section *Construction* in Chapter 6 gives details of how to calculate snow loading.

Tank size and shape
The outer area of a tank (including surface, sides, and base) can be minimised to reduce heat loss:

- A single tank with a large capacity will lose heat less quickly than several smaller ones with the same total storage capacity. This is because its surface area to volume ratio will be smaller in comparison.
- Round tanks have a lower surface area to volume ratio than rectangular ones. Therefore they lose heat less quickly.
- Using straight (non-corrugated) steel sides also reduces the surface area of the tank sides, limiting the rate at which heat is lost.

Ground storage lakes
The issue of the surface area to volume ratio applies to lakes as well as tanks, although the surface through which most of the heat will be lost is the top surface of the water. Therefore an artificial lake should be deep, rather than shallow, to minimise the probability of freezing. Caution is necessary before deepening an existing lake, however; as well as stirring up pollution from the bottom of the lake it is possible to dig through the waterproof layer whereupon the lake may drain. Consultation with qualified engineers is essential if excavation of an artificial lake or modification of an existing lake is to be properly considered as an option for water storage.

---

[17] Alter and Cohen (1969)

3.4 Water treatment

Cold water is more viscous than warm water, and rates of chemical and biological reactions are slower at lower temperatures. Awareness of the effect of these factors will contribute to the implementation of an efficient water treatment regime.

Mixing and pumping requirements

The increased viscosity of water, when cold, affects the energy requirements for mixing water with coagulants and for the power required for pumping operations. Figure 3.7 is a graph showing the correction factor for the effect of temperature on viscosity-dominated processes. This should be used to calculate the extra energy required for pumping or mixing operations involving cold water.

Note that viscosity is often quoted at 20°C, so the correction factor shown for 20°C is 1.0. If water temperature is reduced from 20°C to just above 0°C then the rate of viscosity-dominated processes will be reduced to about 0.57 (= 1/1.75) times that at 20°C and the extra energy required rises accordingly.

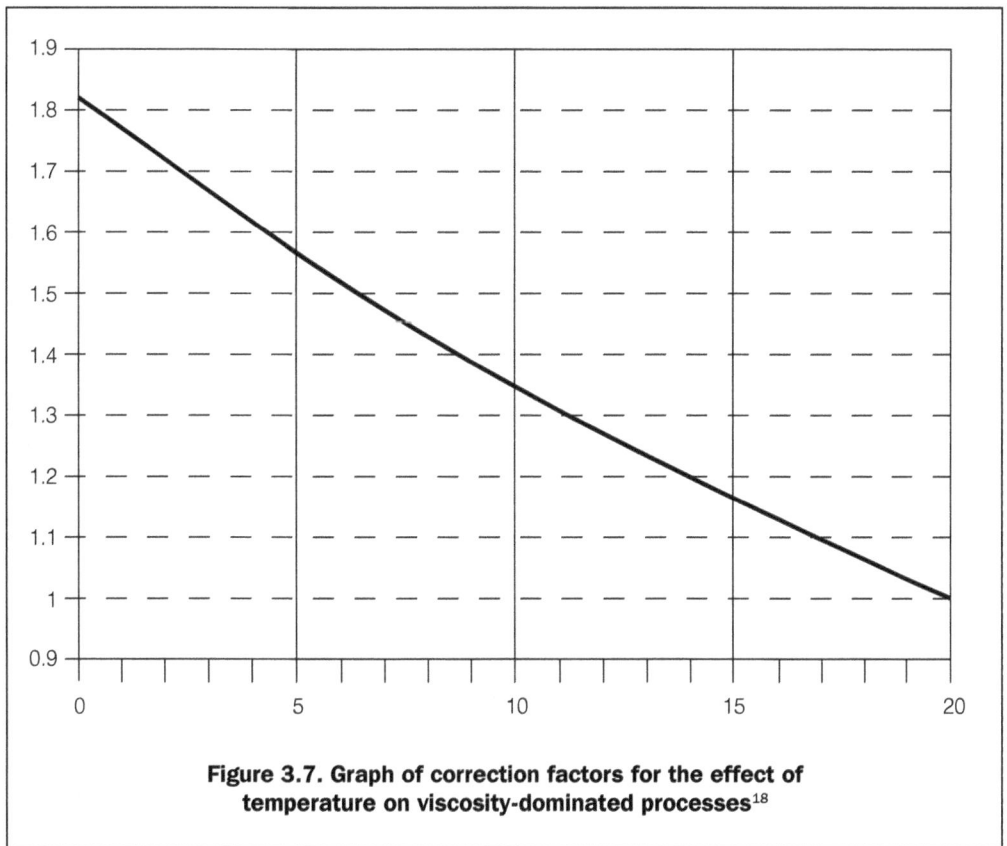

Figure 3.7. Graph of correction factors for the effect of temperature on viscosity-dominated processes[18]

---

[18] adapted from Smith (1996)

Sedimentation tanks

The function of a sedimentation tank is to reduce the turbidity of water by allowing it to deposit suspended solids in the still water of the tank. In emergencies the aim is to produce a water supply with a turbidity of less than 5 NTU in order to maximise the efficiency of the chlorination process, although chlorination will function relatively effectively at turbidities of up to 20 NTU. The design of sedimentation tanks is well explained in *Engineering in Emergencies*[19] and other emergency manuals.

The footprint (area in plan) of a sedimentation tank is often calculated using:

$$\text{Area (m}^2\text{)} = \text{design flow rate (m}^3\text{/s)} \div \text{settlement velocity (m/s)}$$

If the settlement velocity is miscalculated, the wrong size of tank will be built. Therefore to obtain accurate results it is imperative in cold regions that jar tests to determine settlement velocity of suspended solids should be done at the correct (outside) temperature. Similar jar tests, which determine how much alum (or other coagulant) to add to a water system before chemically assisted sedimentation, should also be carried out at the correct (outside) temperature.

Chemical disinfection

Chemical processes are slower in cold water, a prime example being the reaction when water is chlorinated. Some text books on the subject look at the 'CT' value (Concentration of residual disinfectant × contact Time). Authors differ in explaining how the CT value is affected by temperature. Patwardhan[20] states that for every 6°C drop in water temperature the CT value needs to be increased by a factor of between 1.5 to 3.5, while the US Environmental Protection Agency states that to achieve a consistent inactivation of *Giardia Lamblia* the CT values for chlorine need to be approximately doubled for each 10°C drop in water temperature.[21]

In practice, the chlorine quantity and contact time required should be tested at the correct temperature. If not, tank design may allow insufficient contact time, or insufficient doses of chlorine could be added. Proper disinfection of the water would then not be assured.

Filtration

Two factors affect the use of filter beds to treat water in cold regions: the increase in water viscosity causes greater headloss in water flowing through filters, and the reduced rate of bacterial activity at low temperatures affects the operation of slow sand filters.

---

[19] Davis and Lambert (1996)
[20] Patwardhan (1989)
[21] USEPA (1990)

Slow sand filters

Slow sand filtration is usually effective when the biological action of the schmutzdecke (a thin bacterial layer at the top of the sand) efficiently breaks down organic matter. The factor by which the number of *E.Coli* in the water is reduced is normally in the range 100 to 1000, however the factor can be as low as 2 if water temperature is less than 2°C.[22] Chlorination is sometimes used as a further treatment method to disinfect water following slow sand filtration. Depending on how effectively a filter removes faecal coliforms, at low temperatures further treatment by chlorination will almost certainly be necessary.

In conditions where the ambient temperatures are sub-zero there are two approaches to coping with ice forming in filter units:

- Cover filters with a roof and an insulating soil layer to help prevent the formation of ice on the surface of the water to be filtered.
- Design the structure, around the filter, to withstand the expansion forces of the ice. This method has been used successfully in the US, using filter sidewalls of 15cm-thick reinforced concrete, covering earth embankment walls sloped at 1:2.[23] Slow sand filters have been kept running with a floating ice block. Although the rate of removal of *E.Coli* is small, this is effective so long as the ice does not touch the schmutzdecke, the temperature of which should not be allowed to cool below 0°C.

Rapid gravity (roughing) filters

Rapid gravity filtration, or roughing filtration, is effective in cold regions, although head losses through the filter will be increased due to the increased viscosity of the water. Relative head loss increases by 2.5 to 3.5 per cent for each °C that the water temperature is reduced.[24]

Removing glacial flour

One use of roughing filtration is to remove glacial flour from a water supply. Glacial flour is created by the abrasive action of glacial ice rubbing rocks against the bedrock, creating very fine particles that appear as reflective specks in the water. These can be very difficult to remove from the water, however one method is to treat the water with between 10 and 30mg/litre of ferric chloride followed by settling, roughing filtration, or both.[25]

Other factors affecting the removal of glacial flour are:

- Ferric chloride is often more difficult to obtain, and more expensive, than alum, which is the most common coagulant. Other coagulants may also be effective, and it is worth doing jar tests using alum, for example.
- People may already be accustomed to drinking water containing glacial flour. If the water quality is satisfactory in terms of bacterial content, removal of glacial flour may not be necessary.

---

[22] Huisman and Wood (1974)
[23] Hendricks (1991)
[24] Smith (1996)
[25] Ryan (1990)

Boiling water

In cold areas, heaters are obviously necessary for survival and personal comfort, irrespective of water supply or treatment options. If suitable heaters or stoves are widely used or readily available, boiling water may be an effective way to kill disease-causing organisms present in the water. As a disinfection method, boiling is suited to the treatment of small quantities, with each household treating its own drinking water.

For disinfection purposes water should be brought to a rolling (vigorous) boil, and boiling continued for one extra minute for every 1000 metres of altitude above sea level.[26] Alternatively, boil water for between five and ten minutes.[27]

Key factors affecting the suitability of boiling as a method of water disinfection are:

- The amount of fuel available: it takes about 1kg of wood to sufficiently boil each litre of water, depending on altitude.[28] This fuel requirement will be greater still if ambient temperatures are cold. Fuel may be too scarce, and consequently too expensive, to use for water disinfection purposes.
- Local people must be aware both of the required boiling time for effective disinfection, and of hygienic water storage practices.

Table 3.1 shows the effect of altitude on the boiling point of water. Note that the boiling point of water is actually dependent on the air pressure, which is why the estimated air pressure is also shown. These figures are a conservative estimate and if the air pressure at sea level is higher the boiling point of water will also increase.

Table 3.1. The effect of altitude on the boiling point of water[29]		
Altitude (m)	**Pressure (mm of Hg)**	**Boiling point (°C)**
0	760.0	100.0
500	715.4	98.4
1,000	673.7	96.6
1,500	634.9	95.0
2,000	595.8	93.3
2,500	560.0	91.7
3,000	526.2	90.0
4,000	464.3	86.4

---

[26] UNHCR (1982) and Ockwell (1986)
[27] Davis and Lambert (1995)
[28] Davis and Lambert (1995)
[29] Adapted from pump.net (2002)

WATER SUPPLY

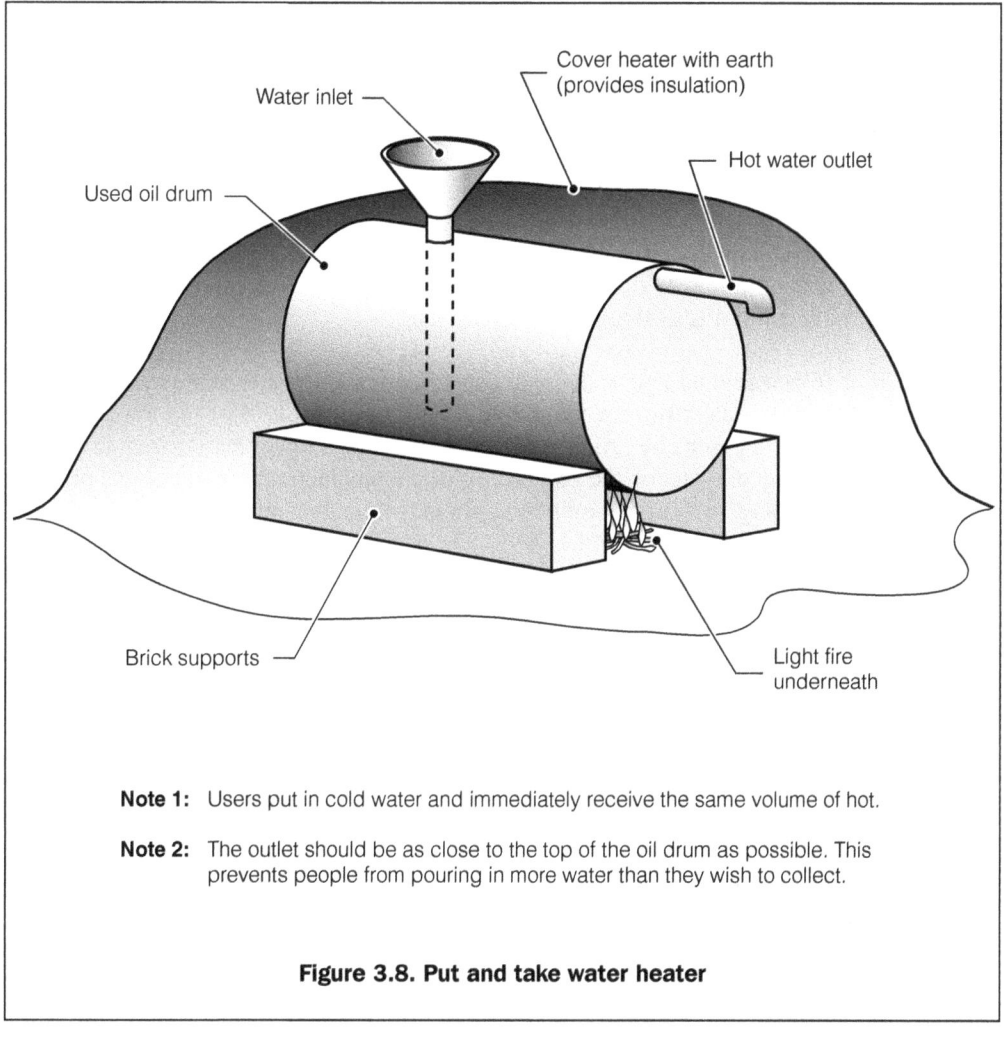

Note 1: Users put in cold water and immediately receive the same volume of hot.

Note 2: The outlet should be as close to the top of the oil drum as possible. This prevents people from pouring in more water than they wish to collect.

Figure 3.8. Put and take water heater

Heating water for washing

When people wash regularly the incidence of contact-related diseases is reduced. Children, especially, will wash more often if hot water is available; washing clothes in hot water is an effective way to kill the eggs of lice (see the section 6.1 *Health*). The provision of hot water facilities for washing, will make a positive contribution to the overall health of refugees in cold areas.

In some areas it is appropriate to provide communal washing and bathing areas. Known as 'hamams' in central Asia, these are usually segregated by sex or have male-only and female-only bathing times. Not only do they allow people to stay clean, in many cultures they are also important as social centres.

For small-scale production of hot water, simple 'put and take' water heaters can be constructed from oil drums, as shown in Figure 3.8.

3.5 Distribution systems

In cold regions distribution systems and pumps are two of the most vulnerable components of a water supply system. Water in pipes is likely to freeze solid, expanding as it does so damaging pipes and causing leakage of water after the pipes have thawed. Pumps are liable to frost damage and may have fuel or electrical power problems.

Leaks

A common problem is detecting leaks. Pipes contracting in the cold make winter the most likely time for tension forces to open poor joints or other weaknesses in the pipe. Locating leaks under frozen ground is difficult for two reasons:[30]

- The cap of frozen ground above the leak can force leaking water sideways rather than upwards. Normally leaks surface via the relatively loose backfill of the trench, and so water flows to the surface close to the problem in the pipe. However in frozen ground the noticeable problem of water on the ground could be many metres from the actual problem in the pipe, leading to false assumptions about where the problem is and, perhaps, missing the problem altogether.
- A thick frost cap can cause sound distortion that makes the use of aquaphones and geophones (leak detection equipment) more difficult.

Leaking pipes will cause a slipping hazard when water comes to the ground surface and freezes.

Preventing pipes freezing

Water freezing in pipes can be avoided by burial, insulation, draining pipes or by maintaining a continuous flow. Selecting the correct pipe material reduces the probability of damage, should water freeze inside.

Draining distribution pipes and tapstands

If pipes have to be laid quickly, for possible burial at a later date, the best way to prevent them from freezing up is to arrange for the pipes to be drained when not in use. Pipes leading from a water source to raw water bulk storage tanks can be drained when water is not being pumped, and arrangements made to drain water out of temporary distribution systems at night.

Where ambient temperatures are at or below −10°C it is worth draining temporary distribution networks at night, even if buried at shallow depth. Two design features will help:

1. Install a vertical air inlet pipe after the outlet gate valve of the water storage tanks or break pressure tanks (see Figure 3.6).
2. Fit washout valves and drainage facilities at low points in the distribution system.

By opening taps at tapstands, all water can be drained from the pipes. In the event of tapstands becoming frozen, people have been observed lighting fires underneath them, causing damage to both the pipes and the wooden posts.

---

[30] Gros (1980)

WATER SUPPLY

Maintaining a continuous flow
One alternative to draining the pipes is to keep water continuously moving inside them.

Either:
- Leave some taps running at distribution points. Adequate drainage facilities will be needed. Note that this is obviously wasteful of water, and would only be used as a temporary solution.

Or
- For a pumped system the water can be recirculated, although it requires that at least two parallel pipes are laid along the entire length through which water is to be pumped, and for several valves and joints to be used (see Figure 3.9).

For both these options, draining the pipes when not in use seems a better long-term option.

Surface-laid pipes
Uninsulated surface-laid pipes are most at risk from freezing. By measuring the air temperature and the temperature of the water entering the pipe it is possible to calculate the approximate values of:

- how long water will take to cool down to the freezing point; and
- the maximum acceptable length for an unprotected surface-laid pipe, for a given flow rate, so that the water in it does not cool to 0°C.

Appendix C shows one method of calculating these values.

Pipe burial
In areas where the ground is not permanently frozen, effective protection against seasonal freezing can be provided by burying most major pipework in the ground. The depth of burial is critical and should, ideally, be greater than the maximum depth of frost penetration. The penetration of frost increases throughout the winter, reaching a maximum sometime after the coldest period of the winter. The maximum depth of frost penetration may be a few weeks, or possibly months after the coldest period.

Deep trenching requires more work than shallow, because when trenches are more than about 80cm deep they can no longer be just one spade-width wide: they must be both wide enough for someone to stand in to dig deeper, and built with sloping sides (for safety reasons). Local workers can be encouraged to ensure the necessary depth of trenching by asking them to use a 'former' frame (made simply of wood) the same dimensions as the required trench cross-section. This way it will be obvious when the trench profile is correct. Substantially more time should be allowed to excavate trenches, of more than 80cm depth.

Local engineers should have some knowledge of the depth of maximum frost penetration. Otherwise it can be determined by digging trial holes, after the coldest part of the winter, and determining at what depth the soil is not frozen by analysing its texture and/or temperature.

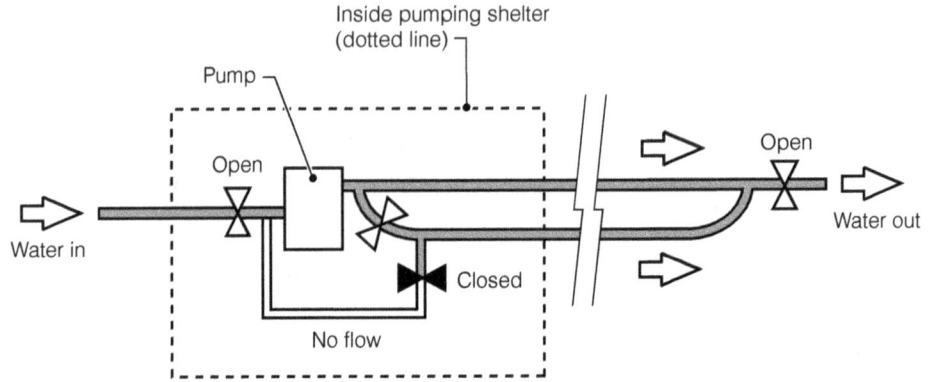

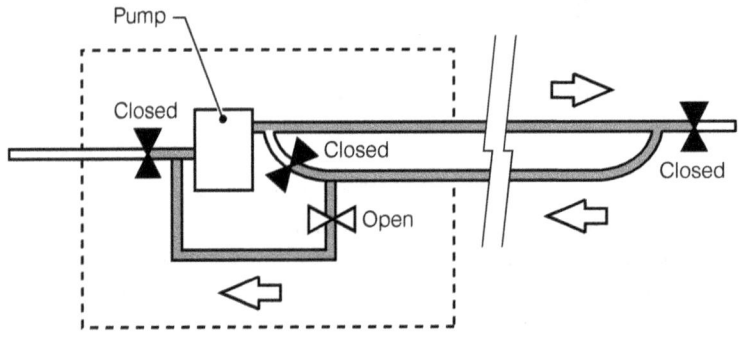

Note 1: Represents a gate which can be opened ⋈ or closed. ⋈

Note 2: When water is not being transferred the pump is run either continually or periodically (severy half hour or so).

Note 3: This system is suitable for short periods where water is not transferred. For longer periods, the pipes and pump should both be drained.

Figure 3.9. Recirculating pumped system

WATER SUPPLY

Pipe insulation
Pipe insulation is effective on its own or in combination with pipe burial. If both methods are employed then the minimum desirable depth is still at least 0.5 to 1.0m, which means that daily air temperature fluctuations will have an insignificant effect, and protection is provided from loads on the ground's surface. In terms of reducing frost penetration a 1.2m wide, 50mm-thick polystyrene-foam insulating board laid directly above a buried pipe is roughly equivalent to 1.2m of sand or silt cover or 1.0m of clay cover.[31] More excavation will be needed for the trench to accommodate the width of the polystyrene boards. Although expensive, pre-insulated HDPE pipes (discussed below) are also suitable for burial.

A North American solution to above-ground pipe insulation is that of a 'utilidor'. Commonly several services, including water supply, sewerage and electricity supply share an elongated wooden or plastic box structure which is filled with insulating foam. A simplified version of this technology is suitable for emergency water supply. The advantage over pipe burial is that pipes are easily accessible for repair. The advantage over simple pipe lagging is that insulation can be thicker and more effective, being protected from rain water.

Disadvantages of utilidors include that in desperate circumstances people will be tempted to use any available wood (such as a utilidor wall) for fuel. Also when a utilidor is required to cross a road it will either have to raised above the level of the traffic or buried.

Pipe materials
Damage to pipes from water freezing inside can be avoided or mitigated by selecting of a suitable pipe material. Appendix B shows the thermal properties of some construction materials, including those used to make pipes.

Medium and high-density polyethylene (MDPE and HDPE)
- Polyethylene remains ductile, even at -60°C, so if water does freeze in the pipes they are unlikely to crack. HDPE pipes have been known to survive several freeze–thaw cycles. Heat-welded joints are also strong enough to resist the pressures of water expansion on freezing.
- MDPE and HDPE have low thermal conductivity, so the insulating effect can mean that water is less likely to freeze in them than in pipes made from other materials, especially metal.
- MDPE or HDPE pipes flexible and sometimes available on long rolls, which also makes them relatively easy to install.

Polyvinylchloride (UPVC)
- UPVC is ductile at 20°C, but can become brittle at very low temperatures (e.g. lower than -10°C) or with prolonged exposure to sunlight.
- UPVC generally having thinner walls than MDPE or HDPE pipes, and so offer less insulation and are more prone to accidental breakage.
- PVC pipes require thrust blocks at changes in pipe direction to prevent ice expansion from pulling the slotted joints apart.[32]

---

[31] Smith (1996)
[32] Davis and Lambert (1995)

- Many different grades of PVC are available, with quality and material properties being highly variable, depending on the quality of the manufacturing process. Therefore imported PVC may be much stronger than locally made pipes.
- Polyethylene pipes are not flexible when cold, especially when outside temperatures are below freezing. If butt-welded joints are to be used in situations where it is necessary to manhandle pipes into position fairly accurately, storage of pipes indoors or in a heated tent should be considered so that the pipes are more manageable and flexible.

Metal
- Ductile iron pipes are very resilient but will also be very expensive since it is likely they will need to be imported.
- Pipes made from iron or steel are prone to corrosion, although various coatings can be applied to minimise the effects.
- Although metal pipes are strong, they can still be damaged by ice forces.
- Small diameter (up to 50mm) metal pipes can be defrosted electrically.

Pre-insulated HDPE pipes
- Pre-insulated HDPE pipes have a factory-fitted polyurethane foam insulation layer, which is usually well protected by a waterproof layer of UPVC on the outside.
- Pre-insulated HDPE pipes are the most effective solution for pipes that must be completely exposed to the air. Common applications are when water or sewage pipelines cross bridges (and therefore cannot be buried).
- Although HDPE pipes are an expensive option, they are also suitable for burial, and can be buried more shallowly than uninsulated pipes as long as there is enough cover to ensure protection from vehicle traffic.

Thermal properties of bare and pre-insulated HDPE pipe are compared in Table 3.2.

Table 3.2. Thermal properties of HDPE pipe, bare and insulated[33]						
Pipe diameter (mm)	Ambient temperature = –18°C			Ambient temperature = –34°C		
	No insulation	With 50mm polyurethane foam		No insulation	With 50mm polyurethane foam	
	Time to freeze (hrs)	Time to freeze (hrs)	Heat loss (w/m)	Time to freeze (hrs)	Time to freeze (hrs)	Heat loss (w/m)
50	1	57	2.7	<1	29	5.0
75	3	107	3.4	1	55	6.5
100	4	149	4.1	2	77	7.7
150	9	241	5.4	5	125	10.2
200	16	333	6.6	8	172	12.4
300	34	530	8.9	17	274	16.8
400	53	692	10.6	27	357	20.0

---

[33] Figures from Urecon Ltd., Quebec, Canada

WATER SUPPLY

Other pipe materials
- Asbestos cement pipes become particularly brittle at low temperatures and should not be used unless permanently and properly buried.
- Acrylonitrile butadiene styrene (ABS) pipes have similar properties to PVC although they require a thicker wall section for the same pressure rating, and are more vulnerable to damage by sunlight.

Defrosting pipes blocked by ice

There are two primary options for defrosting water service pipes to houses that have become blocked by ice. Either a large electric current is passed down metal pipes, warming them up, or hot water is fed into blocked metal or plastic pipes. This subject is discussed comprehensively in 'The Cold Regions Utilities Monograph'.[34] Once some flow has been restored, water passing through the pipes will quickly melt any remaining ice.

Defrosting using electric current
Small-diameter metal pipes, such as those used for connections from water mains to individual houses, can be defrosted by passing a large electric current through them. Welding machines, generators or heavy service transformers may be used to provide the current. Electrical connections should be made to the pipe on each side of the length of pipe to be thawed, so that this length of pipe forms part of the electrical circuit.

Note that this method is potentially dangerous, and adequate safety precautions must be taken, especially to keep people away from live electric cables.

Electrical thawing is only suitable for use with relatively small pipes, from ½-inch (13mm internally) to 2 inches (50mm internally). A typical house connection can be thawed using 300 amps for 4 to 6 minutes. More specific times are given in Table 3.3 while cable sizes suitable for making connections are shown in Table 3.4.

Note that if the current is halved, the time taken will be multiplied by four, since the time taken to defrost is proportional to the heat produced, which is proportional to the amount of electrical power used:

> Electrical power used is given by the equation $P = I^2 R$

where I = electrical current (Amps) and R = electrical resistance of the circuit (Ohms). Larger pipes will have lower electrical resistance, so will take longer to heat up.

The following are also important factors that need to be considered carefully before attempting to use electrical current to defrost water pipes:

---

[34] Smith (1996)

Table 3.3. Approximate current and time for thawing steel pipe[35]

\	Pipe sizes (in inches)						Approximate time (minutes)
½	¾	1	1¼	1½	2		
200	270	400					3-4
150	200	300	400				6-8
125	170	250	340	440			8-12
100	135	200	270	320	440		12-16
75	100	150	200	240	330		25-30
50	67	100	135	160	220		60

Table 3.4. Recommended cable sizes[36]

Amps	Distance from welding machine to pipe connections						
	17	25	33	50	75	100	130
100	2	2	2	1	2/0	3/0	4/0
150	2	2	1	2/0	4/0	4/0	2 of 3/0
200	2	1	1/0	3/0	4/0	2 of 3/0	2 of 4/0
250	2	1/0	2/0	4/0	2 of 2/0	2 of 3/0	
300	1/0	2/0	3/0	4/0	2 of 3/0		
350	1/0	2/0	4/0	2 of 2/0			
400	2/0	3/0	4/0	2 of 3/0			

- Welding machines can only operate at their maximum current rating for about five minutes. If longer times are required the current taken should be no more than 75 per cent of the maximum rating.
- Welding machines generally operate at low voltage (less than 20 Volts). It is the high current, not the voltage, that will heat up the pipes.
- Wide-diameter wire is needed to connect welding machines to pipes. In principle the cross-sectional area of the wire should be greater than that of the metal of the pipe, so that the wire has less resistance and does not get hot.

---

[35] Nelson (1980)
[36] Nelson (1980)

- Make good electrical connections to pipes and check them before turning on the current.
- This method is suitable for underground pipes only, not indoor plumbing, which can be thawed simply by warming up the house.
- Before operation, disconnect earth connections to household plumbing, or disconnect the service pipe altogether, otherwise there is a risk of fire. Remove water meters from the pipe section to be defrosted.
- Current can jump from water pipes to nearby gas pipes, which will reduce the effectiveness of this technique.
- In an emergency, welding machines are likely to be needed for vehicle and building repairs, not just defrosting water pipes. Think carefully before removing them from their normal activities.

Defrosting using hot water
This is suitable for both metal and plastic pipes. A flexible pipe is fed into sections of frozen underground pipe: hot water is continually pumped through the flexible pipe so that it melts the ice that is blocking the pipe.

The main advantage of this method is its simplicity. A 20- to 100-litre water container fitted with a hand-pumping mechanism can be used as a hot water reservoir and refilled from stoves and kettles. Alternatively consider using water directly from the outlet of a domestic water heater somewhere in the building. Another advantage of using hot water is that the method is suitable for any diameter of pipe, whereas using electrical current is only practical for defrosting small diameter metal pipes.

The most common problem with using hot water arises because pipes often have internal obstructions from bends, mineral deposits, valves, and so on. The hot water method is reported to be about 50 per cent successful, on average.

Plumbing of hospitals and collective centres

Figure 3.10 shows a simple and effective way to plumb a several-storey building into a distribution system that supplies water intermittently. This system was used for a hospital in Pristina (Kosovo) in 1999. The simplicity of the system shown in Figure 3.10 means that, once installed, there is very little that cound go wrong provided there is sufficient pressure in the water main at some time during the day.[37]

Important features:
1. The lower check (one-way) valve and the ball-cock valve at the tank will ensure that water is taken from the system whenever it is available.
2. Temporary water tanks should be located in the uppermost intact rooms of the building, rather than on the roof where they may be liable to freezing.
3. Almost any point of an existing cold-water supply system will suffice for the connection from the main water supply.
4. Due to the upper check (one-way) valve, water will flow in different directions at different times in different pipes, but as long as there are no leaks, pressure will be maintained by the temporary storage tank.

---

[37] Reinbold (2000)

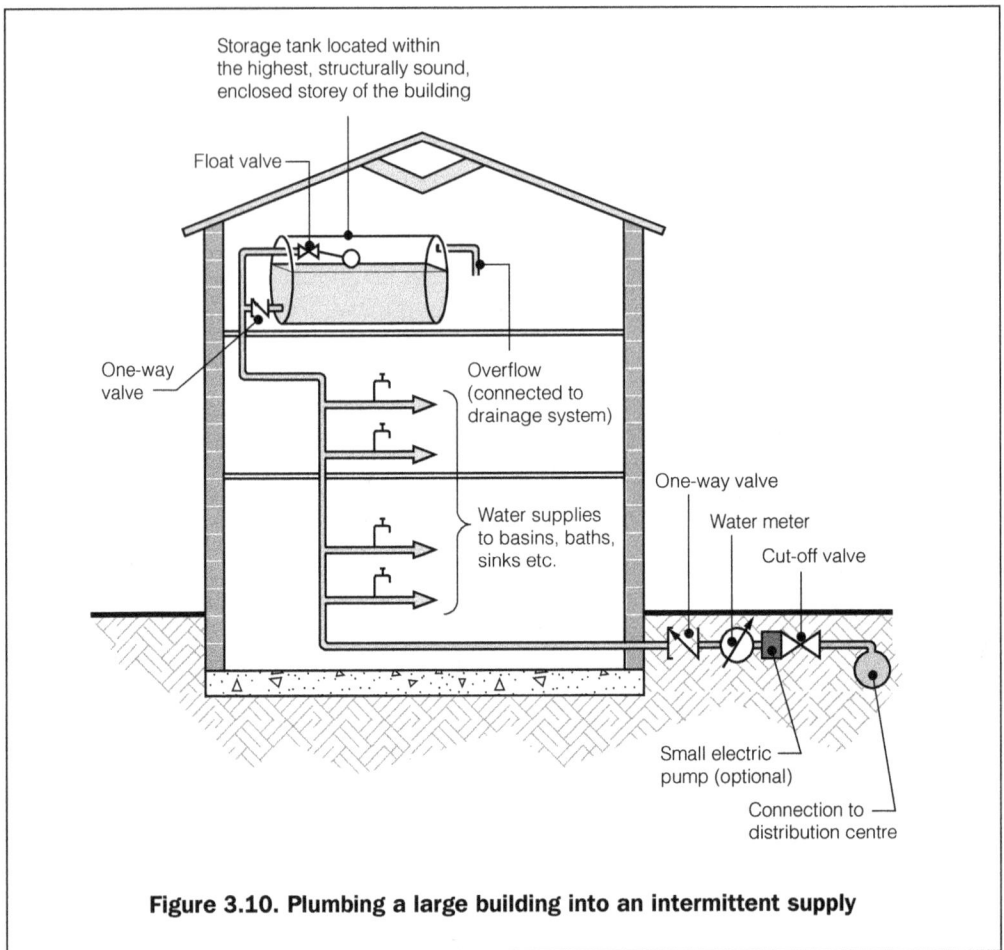

Figure 3.10. Plumbing a large building into an intermittent supply

5. An obvious addition when a water supply has little, or no, pressure for much of the day is a small electric pump, switched on either automatically or manually. Either way, any pump will need some operation and maintenance.

Warning: Structural checks must be made to ensure that the building (floor and walls) can support the weight of the temporary tank or tanks when filled with water.

Protecting distribution points

It is preferable to locate water distribution points inside a shelter for two reasons. First, shelter prevents the problem of water freezing inside standposts or handpumps, and secondly it will provide a more comfortable and safer environment in which people can wait while queuing for water or filling containers.

The location of distribution points in relation to accommodation will obviously affect the length of time that people will have to walk (in cold weather) in order to fetch water. Even a trip of five minute's duration may constitute a serious risk of exposure to old or sick people.

Drainage of water distribution areas
An important consideration for water distribution points, in any climatic region, is how to provide drainage away from the immediate area. In the summertime standing water provides a potential breeding site for insects that transmit disease. In the winter poor drainage will cause a slipping hazard or mud and water will make using the tap very unpleasant.

The construction of a properly drained area, for example a concrete slab draining to a soakaway, will both prevent the health problems associated with puddles of standing water, which can contaminate wells and boreholes, and help to prevent a build-up of ice that poses the immediate hazard of slipping and falling for people using water distribution points.

Protection of simple stand pipes
Simple standpipes can be protected from the cold by using basic insulation, for example by wrapping sacking around exposed pipes, constructing a wooden box around them or by a 'tap box', which is filled with soil in winter and can be removed during the summer for maintenance. Soil in the tap box acts as insulation. This principle is illustrated in Figure 3.9. An improvement to the tap box shown is to put a waterproof roof on it to prevent rain from getting in, since soil containing moisture is less insulating than dry soil.

An alternative to filling a tap box with earth is to place a small heat source, such as a small paraffin heater, inside the box at night.[38]

3.6 Water supply in mountainous regions

In the West walkers frequently make the assumption that mountain streams are safe to drink. Streams are sometimes free from pathogens because the population density in mountainous areas is very low, however if refugees arrive in such an area this is no longer true. Also affecting the quality assessment of surface water in mountainous areas is the fact that *E.Coli* are not reliable indicator organisms for protozoan cysts, including *Giardia* and *Cryptosporidium*, and that infectious parasitic cysts can live in water for up to three months.[39] *Giardia* is certainly capable of existing in cold and mountainous areas: *Giardiasis* is an ailment that commonly affects trekkers in Nepal! Therefore even if water tests show an absence of faecal coliforms there may be potentially fatal diseases present in the water.

In refugee camps in mountainous areas all water should be treated to remove pathogens. A proper and safe water supply system should be designed and implemented.

Water sources and treatment
Groups of refugees have used diverse water sources in mountainous regions, including snow, ice, and glacial meltwater streams. In Northern Iraq in 1991, airdrops were made of water in plastic bottles fixed to pallets. According to observers, some 95 per cent of all bottles were destroyed upon impact with the ground.[40] Some water was transported into that same area, in storage tanks, by helicopter. This was very expensive: at that time each litre of water cost

---
[38] Gould (2001)
[39] tripprep.com (1998)
[40] Cuny (1994)

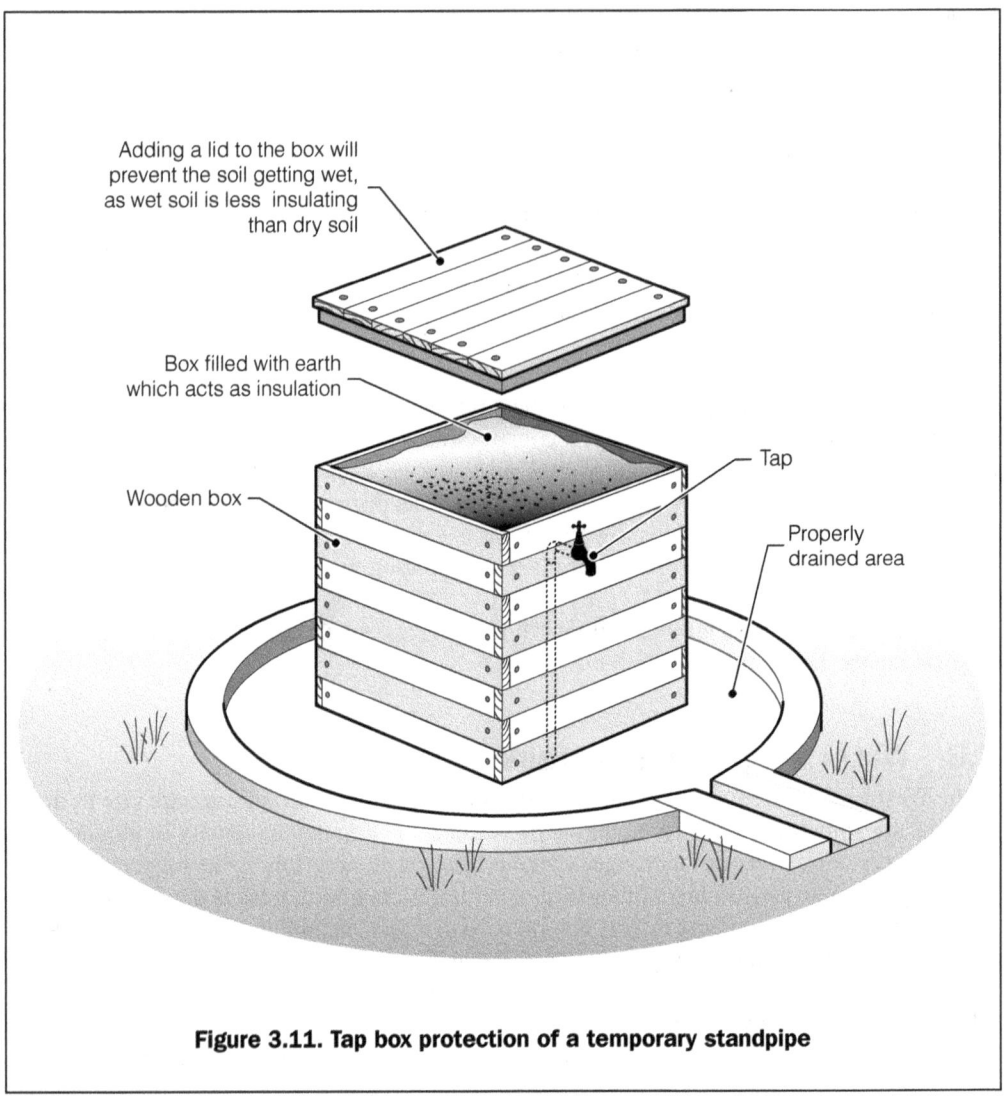

Figure 3.11. Tap box protection of a temporary standpipe

about US$3.50 (in 1991). Therefore careful decisions must be taken concerning which source to use, taking into account the diversity of available sources and the high costs of logistics in mountainous areas. A flowchart to aid water source selection for refugee camps in mountainous areas is shown in Figure 7.2 in Appendix A.

The use and treatment of unusual water sources, including ice and snow, is discussed in detail in the *Water sources* and *Water treatment* sections of this chapter. Also discussed are the effects of altitude on boiling water, and other possible water purification techniques (see section 3.4).

WATER SUPPLY

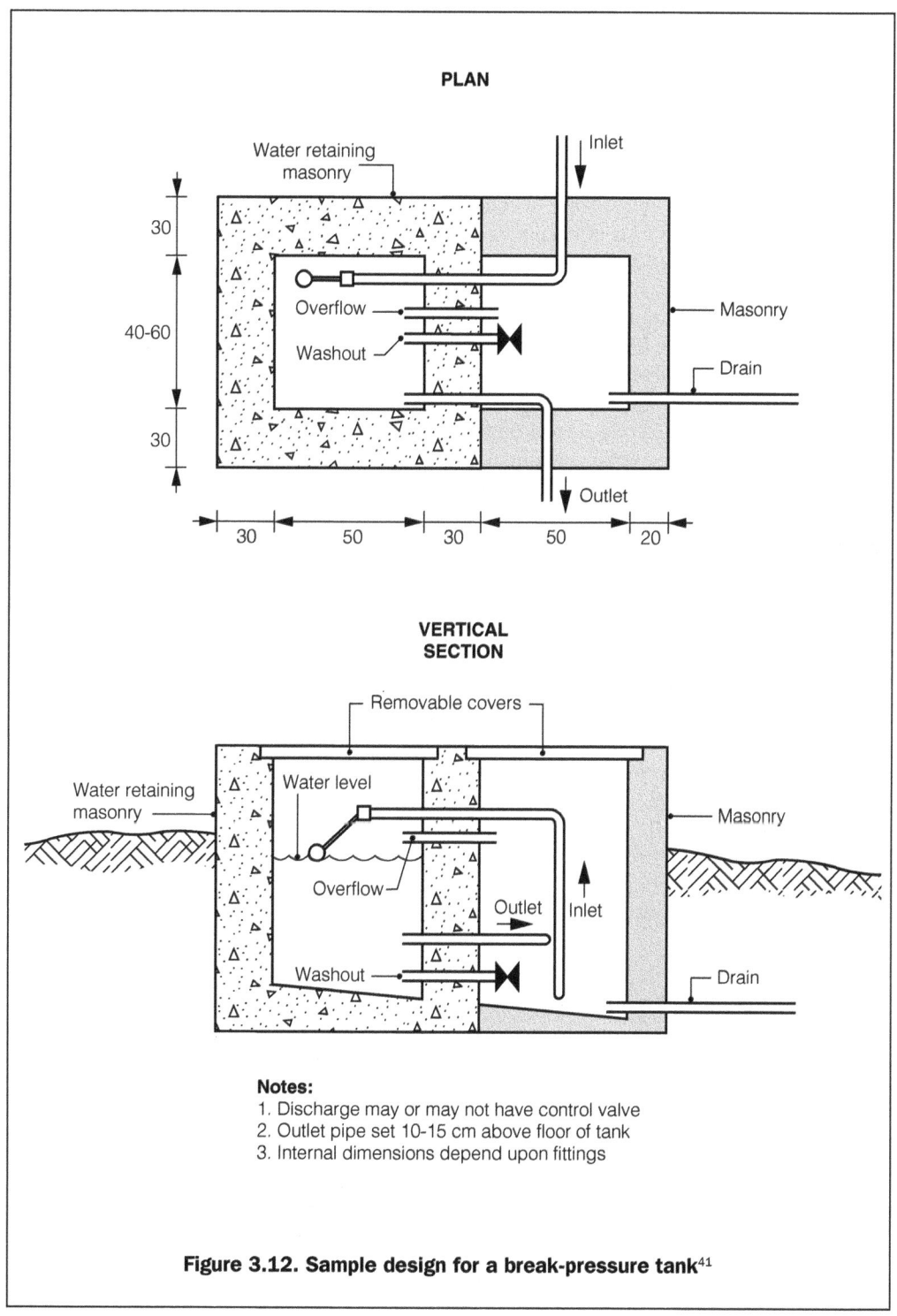

Figure 3.12. Sample design for a break-pressure tank[41]

---
[41] from Smith (1999)

Pressure problems in pipes

Break-pressure tanks

For gravity-fed water supplies flowing over large vertical distances, excessive internal pressures can cause damage to pipes. The maximum internal pipe pressures occur at the lowest points in the system, but break-pressure tanks located above these can help to reduce that maximum pressure. Break-pressure tanks are designed to allow the flow to discharge into a tank with a free water surface in contact with the atmosphere, reducing the hydrostatic pressure to zero, relative to atmospheric pressure. An example of a design for a break-pressure tank is shown in Figure 3.12.

To decide where to position break-pressure tanks it is necessary to understand the theory of hydraulic flow in pipes: this theory is well explained, with examples, in *A Handbook of Gravity-flow Water Systems*.[42]

Pipe deformation due to negative pressure

The opposite problem to excess pressure is that of suction, causing pipes to collapse. If a gate valve at the top end of a water-filled pipe is closed, water is not prevented from flowing out of the lower end, the resulting negative pressure can make even quite substantial pipes (especially plastic ones) collapse. Atmospheric pressure deforms the pipe into an oval or almost flat cross section, from which it does not necessarily recover afterwards. The result for subsequent flow is a greatly reduced flow capacity and loss of pressure head in that section of pipe. Another negative consequence of low pressure inside a pipe is that water containing pathogens may be sucked into the water supply through any small leaks in the pipe, for example at joints. The solution is to turn off the system's gate valves, starting at the bottom and progressing up the hill while keeping the pipes pressurised. If pipes need to be drained down, air must be allowed to enter the pipe at the higher part of the pipe while water is drained out at the lower end.

Pumping at altitude

Centrifugal pumps are better at 'pushing' water than at sucking it, and pumps should be installed so that the suction head (pressure) in the inlet pipe does not fall below a value at which the water will vaporise. Standard water supply manuals cover the principles of pumping.

Two factors decrease the ability of centrifugal pumps to 'suck' water at high altitudes:

1. The reduction in atmospheric pressure directly reduces the height of the water column corresponding to the maximum suction head of the pump.
2. Frictional losses, causing the maximum suction head to be less than atmospheric pressure at sea level, increase at altitude. This is because the water being pumped at altitude will be colder, and therefore more viscous, than the water used for tests at sea level.

---

[42] Jordan (1984)

WATER SUPPLY

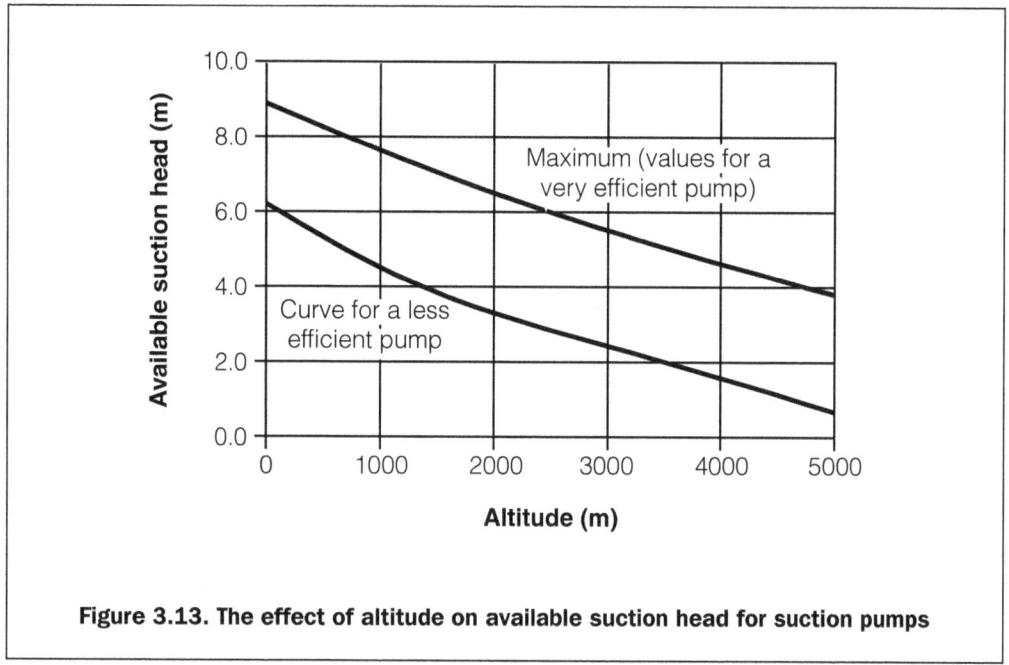

Figure 3.13. The effect of altitude on available suction head for suction pumps

Therefore centrifugal pumps should not be located too far above the water source used, in case the pump has difficulty in functioning. Figure 3.13 shows the likely range of loss of available suction head at altitude, due to loss of pressure and colder water.

3.7 Books on water supply

The following books may be useful to people providing water supplies in emergencies in cold regions:

1. Davis, Jan and Lambert, Bobby, 1995, *Engineering in Emergencies.*
2. House, Sarah and Reed, Bob, 1997, *Emergency Water Sources.*
3. Jordan, Thomas D, 1984, *A Handbook of Gravity-flow Water Systems.*
4. Smith, Dan, 1996, Edited *Cold Regions Utilities Monograph.*

Chapter 4

Sanitation

To control and prevent sanitary related diseases it is important that adequate sanitation, hygiene promotion and safe water supply are implemented together. This is as important in cold regions as it is in the tropics. With this in mind the similarities and differences of providing effective sanitation in cold climates, as opposed to warm or hot ones, are discussed in this chapter.

4.1 Excreta disposal

The importance of hygienic, safe excreta disposal and its relationship with the incidence of faecal-orally transmitted diseases is well established, and covered in some depth in more general guidebooks on emergency water and sanitation, such as those listed at the end of this chapter. In this section the effects of cold weather on pit latrines and open defecation are discussed, as well as some alternative methods of excreta disposal.

Open defecation
Open defecation fields are often suggested as an emergency option for areas with a hot, dry climate. In more temperate or humid conditions, the risk of transmitting pathogens to a new host via the feet of people using the defecation field increases. The desiccating effect of the heat – which keeps pathogenic organisms sealed inside the dry excreta – becomes ineffective, and flow of rainwater spreads faecal material more widely. In sub-zero ambient temperatures the chances of transmitting pathogens via feet decreases again: excreta in open defecation fields quickly become frozen.

In terms of comfort and safety, however, it may be necessary to define a lowest temperature, -10°C for example, below which open defecation is extremely uncomfortable, especially if water is to be used as the method of anal cleansing. Exposure to the cold may result in buttocks becoming frost-bitten.

SANITATION

Pit latrines

In cold regions several factors increase the rate at which sludge builds up in pit latrines, relative to the rate in warmer climates:

- Biological processes, both aerobic and anaerobic, which normally reduce the volume of sludge, effectively halt in sub-zero temperatures. Biological processes restart in the warmer months, provided that temperatures increase to above 0°C; their activity will increase as ambient temperatures rise.
- Frozen ground is largely impermeable. Therefore liquor from the sludge in the pit is not able to soak away in the winter.
- In very cold conditions, with temperatures less than -10°C, excreta falling into the pit may freeze before the pile has time to slump. The pit will not be filled efficiently, instead containing a frozen mound of excreta and void spaces.

The above factors imply that the volume of pits per capita, allocated for sludge storage, needs to be greater in cold regions than in warm ones.

Calculations of pit volume use the formula:[43]

$$V = N \times P \times R$$

where
- V = The sludge storage volume of the pit (m^3)
- N = The effective life of the pit (years)
- P = The average number of people using the pit
- R = The estimated sludge accumulation rate each person (m^3/year)

In cold regions the value of R may be as much as double that of a warm area.

There are benefits to locating pit latrines close to human accommodation, in cold regions. The close proximity will make the latrine more accessible in cold or unpleasant weather and some protection from the accommodation can help to stop cold draughts. Unpleasant smells and flies are minimised best by fitting a tight lid on the latrine opening: water in a water seal, as used in a pour-flush latrine, is likely to freeze during cold periods; a raised vent pipe, as used in a ventilated improved latrine (VIP latrine) will draw cold air into the latrine building. A vent pipe that can be closed in winter may help in areas where summer temperatures make the removal of smells absolutely essential.

Constructing pit latrines in winter

General construction techniques for use in winter are described more fully in Chapter 5. In particular, this includes how to use antifreeze admixes to make concrete suitable for unreinforced latrine slabs. If concrete is not properly cured then it can be structurally weak and liable to collapse.

---

[43] Franceys et al. (1992)

Soil that is hard and structurally sound in winter may go soft in the spring, causing collapse of latrine pits excavated when the ground is firmer. If a latrine pit is dug in winter in frozen ground that is likely to thaw in spring, steps should be taken to prevent the latrine slab from falling in. Extra support can be provided for latrine slabs by embedding two parallel sections of iron pipe, planks or poles into the surrounding soil, making sure they protrude at least 1m on either side of the hole (see Figure 4.1). This spreads the load from the latrine slab over a wider area of soil, including more stable ground than that which is close to the pit sides.

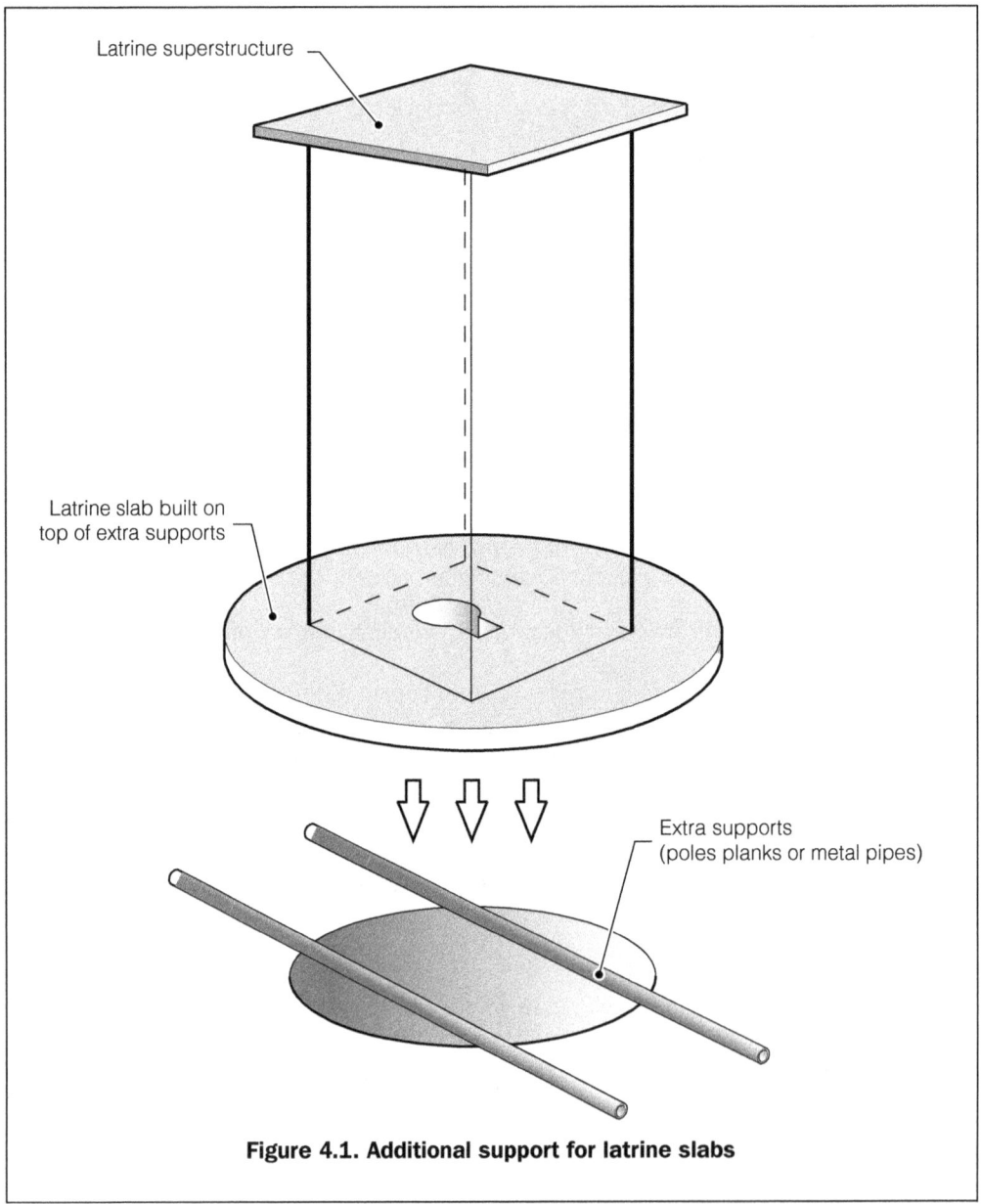

Figure 4.1. Additional support for latrine slabs

SANITATION

Where the soil has been frozen and covered with snow, some aid agencies have successfully used digging machines mounted on the back of snow vehicles to excavate pits. Otherwise normal diggers for construction may be the only option.

Honey-buckets and honey-bags

Established as a solution to excreta disposal problems in rural Alaska, this system is an alternative to pit latrines for when the ground conditions are such that digging pits is impossible. Heavy duty plastic bags, known as 'honey-bags', are used to line bucket latrines.

When a bag is full it is either:

- left under a small shelter outside, where its contents freeze solid. A few weeks later the honey-bags are picked up by a truck and taken to a central wastewater treatment plant; or
- deposited into a larger collection vessel, which is emptied at a later date.

The honey-bag system works well when outside temperatures are very cold (consistently below 0°C) but requires trucks, vehicle access to the area, and a central wastewater treatment facility. Also, with this system, water cannot be used as a method of anal cleansing, as additional unnecessary volume of waste is created: paper has to be used. Therefore in areas where water is the preferred method of anal cleansing, the honey-bag system may not be acceptable for cultural reasons.

Hand-washing facilities

If people and especially children experience discomfort when hand-washing after defecation, that is if the process makes their hands cold, they will be tempted not to wash. Therefore attempts should be made to make this process as pleasant as possible, by:

- periodically pouring hot water into the small water containers that store water for hand-washing at communal latrines, and taking steps to insulate these water containers; and
- providing material for people to dry their hands on: water evaporating off people's hands is what makes them feel cold. Disposable paper is the most hygienic method, although a place to dispose of used paper should be provide, such as a burning pit.

The presence of latrine attendants, on site, would greatly facilitate both the above suggestions.

Figure 4.2 shows a hand-washing facility designed for use in a cold region of China. Heated water is stored in an insulated bucket, and used water is collected in a bowl which can be emptied periodically at a designated drainage or disposal point.

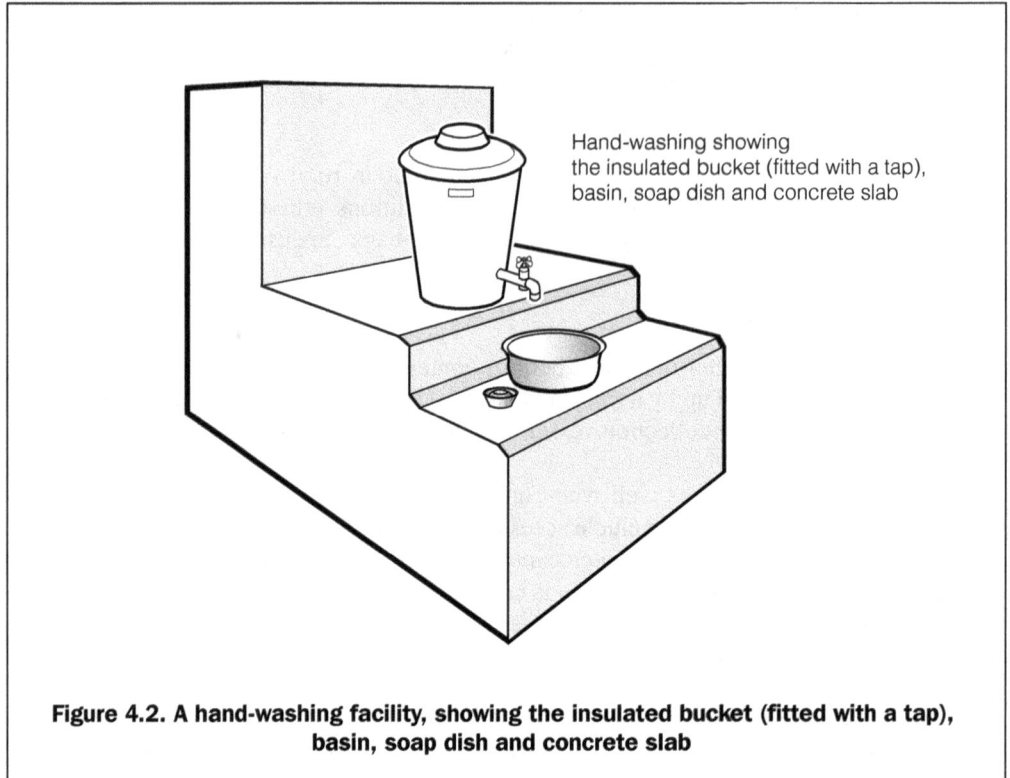

Figure 4.2. A hand-washing facility, showing the insulated bucket (fitted with a tap), basin, soap dish and concrete slab

4.2 Conventional sewerage systems

As with the provision of a water supply, in areas where infrastructure existed before the disaster, the first priority should be to renovate the old system, partly just to prevent further decay.

Experienced engineers are necessary to renovate urban sewerage properly. Some measures that are applicable to repairing sections of sewerage include the:[44]

- rapid repair of sewers, with temporary arrangements to by-pass damaged sections;
- cleaning and flushing of blocked sewers and the treating of sewers with strong disinfectants to prevent the spread of pathogens and limit smells from broken manholes and sewers;
- dewatering of wastewater treatment plants or pumping stations awaiting repair, and arranging temporary haulage of sewage to a burial site or other treatment plant; and
- providing temporary measures, e.g. pit, trench or borehole latrines, aqua-privies and possibly urinals. Use of a honey-bag system may also be appropriate where ground conditions do not suit pit latrines (see section 4.1).

---

[44] adapted from Assar (1971)

SANITATION

Wastewater treatment

As many countries in colder regions of the world have developed infrastructure, wastewater treatment facilities may exist even in rural areas. Therefore a brief description of conventional wastewater treatment methods is relevant here, in addition to descriptions of more basic methods of excreta disposal. Useful books on the theory of wastewater treatment are *Wastewater Engineering*[45] and *Small and Decentralised Wastewater Management Systems*[46].

Large-scale wastewater treatment

Although non-engineering aid workers would be ill-advised to attempt to design wastewater treatment systems, some knowledge of the basic principles involved may be useful when dealing with local engineers and contractors. This section gives a general overview of the processes involved. Figure 4.3 shows the likely flow of wastewater through a conventional treatment works and the sequence of treatment stages. Some of the processes are described briefly below.

Activated sludge (secondary, aerobic process)

Activated sludge is a secondary treatment where bacteria and protozoa feed on the organic matter within wastewater. The active organisms require oxygen from air which is bubbled through the wastewater, or mixed in by fast-spinning aeration rotors partially immersed in the wastewater. The organisms are dispersed throughout the wastewater, and are kept in suspension by the mixing provided by the aeration system. Afterwards, the mixture undergoes a sedimentation process which separates the water from the sludge, which is comprised of the organisms that feed on the organic matter. Some sludge is recycled to start the activated sludge process anew, the rest may be dried, incinerated, or treated further in an anaerobic digester unit. Much sludge is eventually applied to farmland.

Rotating biological contactors (RBCs) (secondary, aerobic process)

In this process wastewater flows past several slowly rotating disks that are half-submerged in the liquid. Biological predators (bacteria and protozoa) live attached to the disks, which rotate so that oxygen is taken into the layer of water covering the part of the disks which is exposed to the air. The bacteria and protozoa need the oxygen to respire, so it is bad for the process if the disks stop turning (although very slow rotation is satisfactory).

Percolating filters (secondary, aerobic process)

This is a common alternative to the activated sludge process. By a moving arm wastewater is trickled over gravel beds by a moving arm and is collected from the bottom of the bed. Bacteria and protozoa live on the surface of the gravel, and feed on organic matter in the wastewater. Spaces in the gravel allow air to get to the bacteria and protozoa, and the gravel provides a surface to which the active organisms attach themselves.

Anaerobic sludge digestion

This is a means of treating the solids (sludge) removed during sedimentation stages. Bacteria that can survive without oxygen break down organic matter in an anaerobic (no oxygen) environment in a tank. One product of the reaction is methane, which is often used as a fuel to heat the anaerobic digestor because the process is most effective at warm temperatures.

---

[45] Metcalf and Eddy (1991)
[46] Crites and Tchobanoglous (1998)

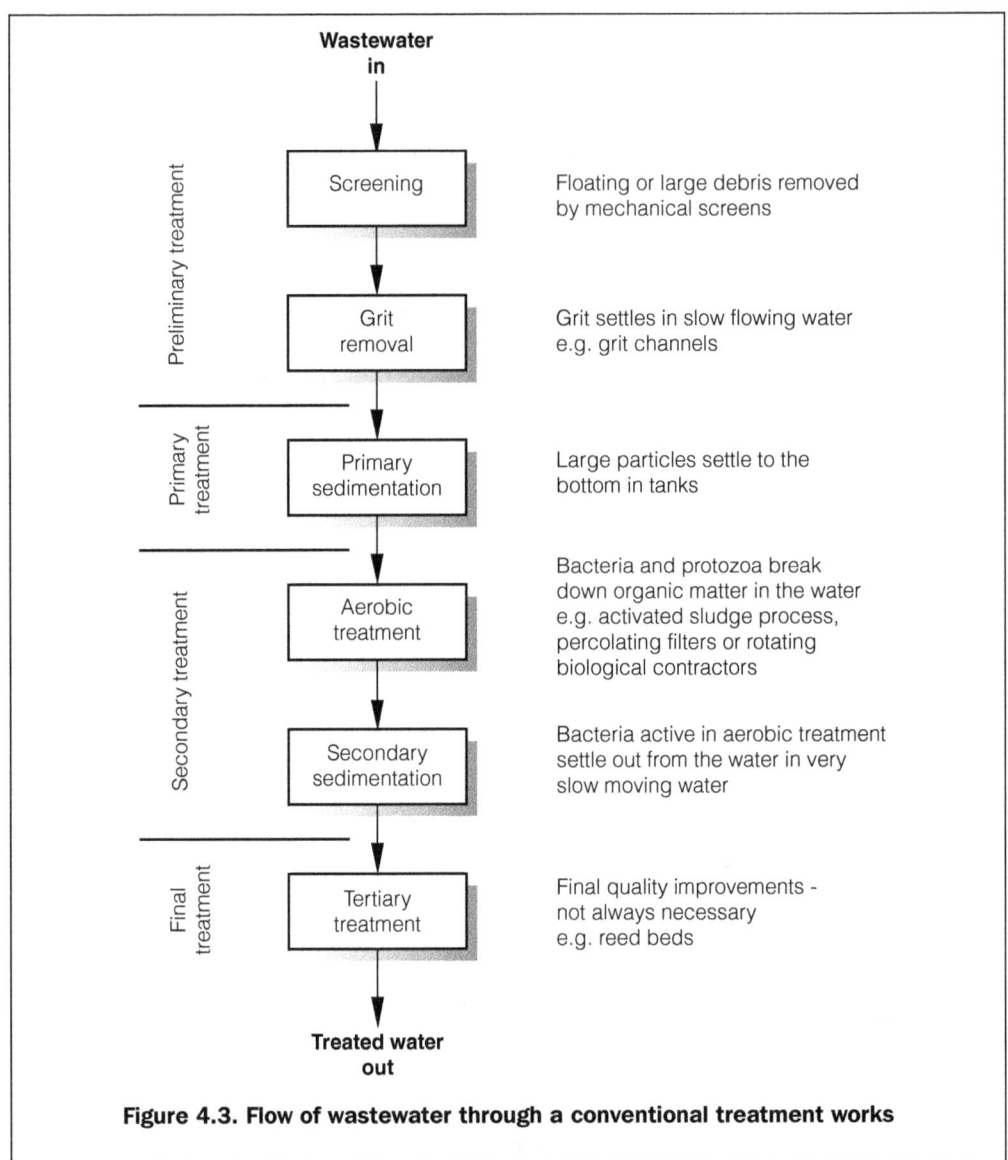

Figure 4.3. Flow of wastewater through a conventional treatment works

Wastewater stabilisation ponds
Stabilisation ponds are used in some cold countries as an alternative to conventional treatment facilities. Facultative or anaerobic ponds are the most suitable, since fully aerobic ponds (maturation ponds) are shallower, and are therefore more likely to freeze. If freezing is inevitable, it is worth noting that a shallow, aerobic pond will warm more quickly in the springtime, allowing treatment to recommence as bacterial activity increases. Aerated lagoons, consisting of large lagoons in which spinning rotors (surface aerators) are installed, can provide more rapid treatment, but require skilled staff and mechanical and electrical equipment. Ponds need a holding capacity large enough to store wastewater for the whole winter, because biological action effectively halts at less than 0°C.

SANITATION

The discharge rate of treated wastewater from a system of ponds is designed to be equal to the rate of treatment of the wastewater. However in the warmer months this rate will be greater than the rate in the winter, when the rate of treatment is negligible.

The following rough calculation relates the necessary average summer treatment rate to the mean rate of inflow of wastewater, all of which is merely stored during the winter months. If the inflow is constant throughout the year, at flow Q (m³/day) then:

Winter treatment rate = 0 (zero) m³/day

Design treatment rate for **summer** = $Q \times (1 + N_w/N_s)$ m³/day

---

where N_w = Number of winter months
       N_s = Number of summer months

The summer treatment rate will, however, vary. After winter there will be a large volume of wastewater to be treated, but treatment rates will be slow until temperature increases further. Treatment will be most rapid during the warmest months and rates will slow down again as winter approaches.

Small-scale wastewater treatment
Small-scale wastewater treatment systems that aid workers may potentially use or encounter include septic tanks, portable aerobic units, and package plant treatment units.

Septic tanks
Septic tanks provide partial treatment of wastewater in anaerobic conditions (without oxygen) at ambient temperatures (i.e. with no heating). Treated effluent normally goes to a soakaway in the ground.

The use of septic tanks remains viable in temperatures above 0°C. However the rate of sludge accumulation is very high at low temperatures, when the rate of bacterial reaction processes is considerably reduced. Regular desludging is an absolute necessity in cold regions, with sludge being taken either to a wastewater treatment facility or to a designated disposal site.

Portable aerobic units
Self-contained wastewater treatment units that consist of rotating biological contactors in a glass-reinforced plastic shell are manufactured by Klargester and Clearwater in the UK (see section 7.4). Usually the units are semi-submerged in the ground, which provides structural support, although Klargester have also produced a version mounted inside a container unit that the British army have used in Bosnia.

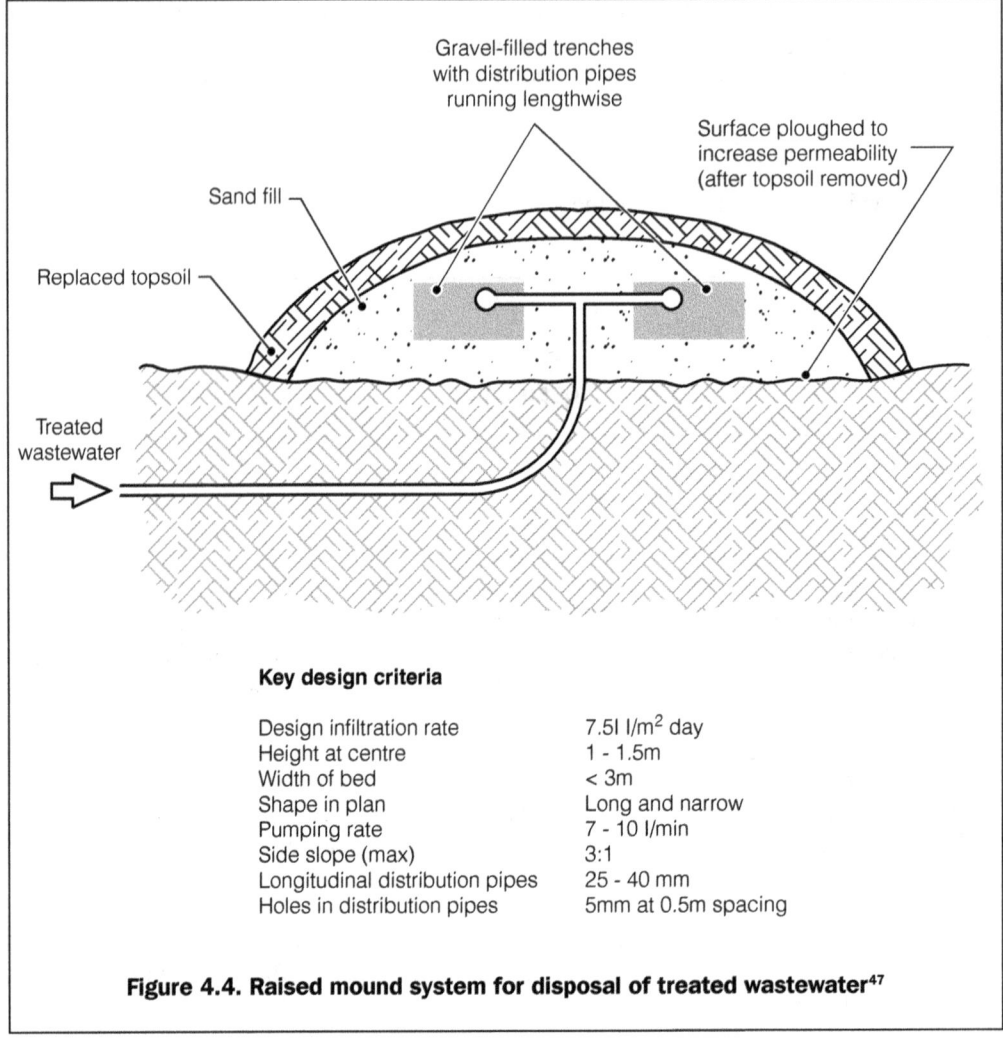

Figure 4.4. Raised mound system for disposal of treated wastewater[47]

Disposal of treated wastewater from small-scale units
Disposal of treated wastewater may be difficult due to frozen ground. One solution is the raised mound system, where treated effluent is pumped into gravel-filled trenches that distribute it evenly along the length of such a mound. Effluent soaks down quickly into the soil below because:

- the mound is constructed from highly permeable sand;
- treated waste is pumped in batches to retain as much heat as possible in the mound; and
- the ground surface underneath is protected from frost by the mound and the surface is prepared by ploughing to help break up large clods of earth.

The mound system is illustrated in Figure 4.4.

---

[47] adapted from Easson et al. (1988)

SANITATION

4.3 Solid waste management

In many ways the disposal of solid waste in cold regions is exactly the same as in warmer ones. In terms of collection, however, the increased logistical difficulties of a severe winter may mean that regular collection is not possible if the available vehicles are badly suited to driving in snow, or if operators are reluctant to perform the service at the coldest time of year. To avoid the random dumping of wastes and to protect the environment, it is advisable to establish a series of local dumping areas that can be cleared in the spring.

Disposal of solid waste in landfill sites may or may not be possible in winter due to frozen ground and unavailability of suitable digging equipment. Burning solid waste may be the best solution, if substances that would produce dangerous fumes or residues are separated from other materials and not burned.

If honey-bags are used as a method of excreta disposal in rural areas, a special area in the village dump should be allocated for their winter storage. Before the winter ends (and the bags begin to thaw), honey-bags should be either removed for treatment or emptied into a watertight storage lagoon or tank from which wastes can be transported by tanker for treatment.

4.4 Disposal of the dead

In addition to the usual considerations of burial and cremation, low temperatures will have both positive and negative implications on this process.

On the positive side:
- the cold will reduce the rate of biological decay processes;
- low temperatures will suppress unpleasant smells; and
- any unheated building can be used as a morgue.

On the negative side:
- cremation could be impractical since fuel may be extremely valuable during a time of disaster;
- burial may also be difficult due to hard, frozen ground; and
- pathogenic organisms may survive for long periods (even years) within or in close proximity to corpses.

4.5 Environmental sanitation in mountainous areas

Excreta disposal in mountainous areas

Accessibility, the hardness of the ground, and the availability of materials will all affect the excreta disposal options that are suitable for mountainous areas. Some useful points are:

- As in all refugee camps, latrines or defecation areas should be located downhill of the camp at the earliest possible opportunity.
- Pit latrines are an option only if it is logistically feasible to supply a few basic materials (for screens and slabs) to the area, and if the ground is not too hard.

- If materials can be brought into the area, but the ground is too rocky or hard to dig pits, raised platform latrines can be constructed above natural hollows.
- If access to the area for trucks or tractors is possible, and the temperatures are consistently below 0°C, a honey-bag system (see section 4.1) could be organised. The honey-bag system also avoids the pollution of surface water with faecal material, which inevitably results from the use of raised platform latrines or open defecation.

Solid waste and mountain camps
Arrangements for collection and disposal of waste in mountainous regions need to be very simple, involving the hand-picking of rubbish, that is issuing people with plastic bags to collect refuse and carry it to a central burning or collection area. Factors to consider include:

- Airdrops produce large volumes of solid waste which will be widely scattered.
- Transport to and from mountainous areas is incredibly expensive. Burning waste in situ may be more feasible.
- Collection of waste from some areas will be dangerous because of either natural (such as avalanches, rockfalls) or manmade (such as mines or unexploded armaments) hazards. It may be immoral to ask people to collect from those areas.

In Northern Iraq, firefighters who were part of British mobile support teams successfully involved children in solid waste collection by turning it into a game!

4.6 Books on sanitation
The following books may be useful to people providing sanitation in emergencies in cold regions:

1. Assar, M, 1971, *Guide to Sanitation in Natural Disasters*
2. Easson, M, et al., 1988, *Sanitation Technologies for Temperate and Cold Climates*
3. Franceys, R, et al., 1992, *A Guide to the Development of On-site Sanitation*
4. Davis, Jan and Lambert, Bobby, 1995, *Engineering in Emergencies*
5. Metcalf and Eddy, 1991, *Wastewater Engineering*
6. Smith, Dan, 1996, Edited *Cold Regions Utilities Monograph*
7. Harvey, P.A., Baghri, S. and Reed, R.A., 2002, *Emergency Sanitation*
8. Crites and Tchobanoglous, 1998

Chapter 5

Related technical issues

5.1 Construction

Using concrete in freezing temperatures
In cold regions, concrete structures (slabs, walls) can suffer from a lack of strength caused by small cracks in the material. These cracks form while the concrete is curing, due to ice expansion within the concrete material. Seasonal variations in temperature may result in further weakening of such structures. It is worth bearing in mind that local construction contractors and builders should be competent at making concrete of reasonable quality in the prevailing conditions, and their skills are worth using.

Methods of improving the quality of concrete, by altering the curing process, are suggested here.

Heat addition
If the concrete is kept warm, it reaches a 'critical hardness' before its temperature falls below freezing. The concrete can then be allowed to cool without any significant loss of strength resulting from the expansion of contained water turning into ice. There are several ways to keep concrete warm:[48]

- Construct components (e.g. latrine slabs) indoors or, for in situ concrete, construct a shelter so that the whole area can be heated to above 0°C.
- Mix in situ concrete using warm water, then cover formwork with insulation to retain heat (known as 'thermos curing').
- Heat formwork by means of electrical wires. Alternatively heat the concrete itself by burying in the mixture resistance wire, which can be warmed electrically.

These methods are expensive since they require additional resources, materials and facilities, and use a lot of energy.

---
[48] Krylov (1998)

Antifreeze admixtures

Antifreeze chemicals can be added to the concrete while mixing the dry ingredients. These chemicals prevent the water in the mix from becoming solid ice and expanding in the spaces between aggregate particles before the critical hardness is reached. With their addition the concrete can cure properly.

There are many chemical compounds that lower the freezing point of water, but most will upset the chemical processes taking place inside concrete as it cures. Sodium nitrate ($NaNO_3$), potassium carbonate (K_2CO_3), potassium chloride (KCl) and sodium chloride ($NaCl$) are all possible antifreeze admixtures.

Antifreeze admixtures force the water within the concrete to remain at least partially liquid until the temperature falls below the 'eutectic point', the temperature at which no matter how much antifreeze is added, the solution will completely freeze. The temperature of the eutectic point varies depending on which compound is used. Because some ice crystals form at temperatures above the eutectic point, the operating range for each mix is usually limited to temperatures a few degrees higher than the eutectic point.[49]

Unreinforced concrete (for dome-shaped latrine slabs)

One of the cheapest and most common antifreeze admixes is sodium chloride (table salt). Its eutectic point is at -21°C, so it should be safe to use where the minimum daily temperature does not fall below -15°C. However, chlorides are highly corrosive to steel reinforcing bars, so while acceptable for unreinforced concrete, they cannot be used in reinforced concrete.

Concrete made with an admixture of sodium chloride is suitable for making unreinforced latrine slabs in subzero temperatures down to -15°C. In colder regions calcium chloride, which has a eutectic point of -55°C, could be used. Chlorides should be added at between 5 per cent and 10 per cent of the dry mixture by weight. While curing, latrine slabs should be covered with a tarpaulin to prevent the wind-chill effect from lowering the concrete temperature even more.

Reinforced concrete

Sodium nitrate and potassium carbonate (Potash) are non-corrosive to steel reinforcing bars. Recommended amounts to add depend on the ambient temperature, and are shown in Table 5.1 as a percentage of the weight of the dry cement.

As with unreinforced concrete, structures should be covered with tarpaulins while curing, so that wind-chill cannot cool them to below the ambient temperature.

Insulating concrete

Insulating concrete is used in Alaska as insulation for buried pipes that may be prone to stress, for example under a road. It can also be used as a base for water tanks to prevent loss of heat, or to maintain the structural integrity of frozen ground.

---

[49] Krylov (1998)

Table 5.1. Amount of antifreeze admix added to concrete, by percentage of dry cement weight[50]

Admixture	Minimum daily temperature (°C)	Admix added (% weight of dry cement weight)
Sodium nitrate ($NaNO_3$)	0 to -5	4 to 6
	-6 to -10	6 to 8
	-11 to -15	8 to 10
Potassium carbonate (K_2CO_3)	0 to -5	5 to 6
	-6 to -10	6 to 8
	-11 to -15	8 to 10
	-16 to -20	10 to 12
	-21 to -25	12 to 15

Insulating concrete can be made using polystyrene beads, pumice or expanded shale as the aggregate, instead of gravel. This produces a lightweight mix with high strength and thermal resistance[51]. The density and thermal properties of insulating concrete are shown in Appendix B.

Building on frozen ground

Properties of soil can differ greatly during different seasons. Frozen ground is fairly stable structurally, but it may become very weak and unstable when it thaws in spring or summer. Ground instability can cause the walls and floors of buildings to crack or subside.

In winter, construction on top of soil banks, which are liable to subside or collapse in the spring, should be avoided. Ground which is frozen in the winter but could become marshland when winter ends should also be avoided. Consultation with local people should establish this fact; plants growing in the area could also indicate of seasonal marshland.

Water tanks are especially likely to face problems of structural damage. First because they are very heavy, and secondly they need to be located on high ground. Building water tanks on a bank of earth may appear to be a good idea in winter but it could lead to disaster in the spring. Thirdly, the relatively high temperature of stored water can melt frozen ground in contact with the tank, causing collapse. The design of water storage tanks is discussed in detail in section 3.3.

---

[50] Figures from Krylov (1998)
[51] Smith (ed., 1996)

In general there are three factors affecting construction on hard, frozen ground which is not necessarily frozen in the summer:

1. Mechanical digging equipment may be necessary. SIDA (Swedish International Development Agency) has, in the past, used mechanical digging equipment mounted on snow vehicles.
2. Ground may become unstable in the spring/summer. Particular care is necessary when constructing at the top of slopes or on ground that could be marshy in the summertime. Use local knowledge to determine where it is safe to build.
3. Construction work is best done in the summer although, obviously, this will not always be possible. Unfrozen ground is much easier to work, and it can easily be established whether the ground is strong enough to support structures. In addition, construction materials may be more easily available at warmer times of the year due to better logistical links.

Frost jacking
After several years the action of repeated freezing and thawing of the ground can force piles and telegraph poles to start rising out of the ground. One method of avoiding this is to wrap piles in several layers of plastic sheeting to allow the soil to move independently of the piles. Borehole casings are also liable to frost jacking, the effects of which can be alleviated by using bentonite as annular grouting instead of concrete. Bentonite grout, not concrete, should be used in the annular space around borehole casings. Concrete forms strong bonds with casing steel, and frost jacking of the concrete can then pull sections of casing apart, damaging the structure of wells and boreholes.

Calculating snow loads
Roof structures must be able to support the weight of snow that settles on them. The following equation can be used to calculate the load:[52]

$$L = F \times H \times D \times A$$

where L = total load exerted on the roof (kg)

F = footprint (plan area) of the roof (m²)

H = maximum expected depth of snow on the ground (m). Use the 30 or 50-year expected maximum depth of snow if designing a structure for long-term use.

---

[52] Figures and theory from Boyd (et al., 1981)

> D = density of snow (kg/m³). Old snow with a density between 200 and 400kg/m³ weighs more than new snow with a density of as little as 100kg/m³. Canadian design criteria use D = 240kg/m³ but an attempt should be made to determine a local value if possible.
>
> A = conversion factor taking into account that roofs are generally more exposed than the ground, hence higher wind speeds over them cause less snow to settle. In Canada A = 80% (0.8) is used for general calculations of flat or sloping roofs or A = 60% (0.6) is used for roofs in very exposed areas.

5.2 Logistics

The effects of cold climates on aid provision are accentuated in winter, one of the main reasons being the effect of the weather on logistics. In some areas road and rail links are liable to closure due to snow blockage, and air support may be hampered by foul weather. In other areas frozen lakes may provide landing sites for aircraft, and roads that are poor in the summer may be better to drive on when frozen.

This section deals with the implications of winter logistics with respect to water supply options and other issues. Some recommendations for vehicle maintenance are given in section 5.3.

Water haulage

Hauling water by truck is not possible if roads are blocked with snow, or if ice makes the trip too dangerous for the driver. The effect that this will have on water supply will be that the emphasis must be on using very local sources of water, despite the fact that the quality of these sources may be less than ideal. Therefore, in some cold regions the option of expensive treatment of poor quality water is preferable to hauling in water by truck, which may be simply impossible.

Stockpiling for winter

Problems of bringing diesel fuel into an area by road will affect the ability of agencies to run their vehicles and pumps; similarly fuel for heating and cooking purposes could be more scarce in winter due to transport difficulties. Therefore it is worth considering, carefully, whether it is feasible to stockpile quantities of fuel before winter arrives, tackling the problems of storage, security, and distribution.

Materials worth stockpiling include fuel, medical supplies, building materials, water treatment chemicals, bags to contain wastes, and other hardware that may be needed to implement repairs to water supply or sanitation systems.

Use of vehicles for personal transport

Obviously, vehicles for the transport of personnel or materials need to fulfil requirements necessary for summer and winter driving. Four-wheel drive vehicles offer distinct advantages in mountainous areas in winter, and in other areas where the quality of roads is poor.

In terms of safety, personnel should not set out in winter without:

- snow chains and shovels, in case the vehicle becomes stuck;
- food, water and four-season sleeping bags, in case the driver and passengers have to stay out all night or longer; and
- leaving information with colleagues about travel plans.

The value of keeping warm should not be underestimated. Besides being more comfortable, personnel will also work more efficiently. Cab heating and tea-making facilities are important and should not be considered luxuries.

Chemical control of snow and ice on roads

The purpose of applying chemicals and abrasive materials (such as sand or grit) to road surfaces is to increase the friction between the wheels of vehicles and the road surface, reducing the possibility of skidding. Vehicle journeys are made safer, and the stopping distances that vehicles require are reduced.

Abrasives and/or chemicals should only be applied to a relatively thin covering of ice or snow, such as that created after a snowplough has initially cleared the road of snow, or to an icy surface created when ambient temperatures fall below 0°C after rain. If applied to thicker layers of snow and ice, the abrasives and/or chemicals are likely to become dispersed and less concentrated, reducing their effectiveness. Advantages and disadvantages of applying chemicals and abrasives are shown in Table 5.2.

The quantities of chemicals recommended for ice control and snow removal are shown in Table 5.3. These quantities are designed to produce a 30 per cent melt within 30 minutes of the beginning of snow accumulation.

Side effects of using chemicals to treat roads

It should be noted that the use of chemicals has some adverse side affects, particularly on the environment, so they should be used sparingly and only when necessary. These include:

- damage to certain species of plants;
- potential pollution of shallow wells, ponds or streams that are used as water sources;
- reduction in soil fertility in the surrounding area;
- corrosion of concrete reinforcement, if the concrete is permeable; and
- corrosion of vehicles, if damaged surface coatings expose raw metal.

Table 5.2. Advantages and disadvantages of chemicals and abrasives[53]

Material applied	Main advantages	Main disadvantages
Sodium chloride (rock salt) NaCl	Effective between 0°C and -9.5°C Immediate traction Salt particles quickly bore through the ice layer Low cost	Ineffective below -12.3°C Low rate of solution
Calcium chloride, $CaCl_2$	Effective down to -29.1°C High rate of solution Liberates heat on dissolving	High cost Pavement remains wet afterwards
Mixtures of NaCl and $CaCl_2$	Effective down to -17.9°C Faster than either chemical applied alone	High cost Pavement stays wet longer than with $CaCl_2$
Mixtures of abrasives and chemicals	Effective In very cold weather Immediate improvement in skid resistance if clean ploughing is impossible Free flowing material No freezing of stockpiles Abrasive anchored to the road	Clean-up problems in the springtime May not remove all ice and snow, depending on amount of chemical added Damage to vehicles at high speed from abrasive particles
Abrasives	Immediate improvement to skid resistance	As with abrasive and chemical mixtures (above) Easily brushed off road by tyres

---

[53] From Keyser (1981)

Table 5.3. Recommended applications of chemicals to paved roads with an average daily traffic of 500 vehicles or more[54]

Air Temperature (°C) and road conditions	Application — before snowfall or freezing rain	– to melt loose snow (per cm depth)	– to clean up thin crusts after ploughing	– to clean up thick crust of hard snow or ice
a) -4 or higher, in shade b) -7 to -4, in sun	55 to 115kg of NaCl or mixture (if NaCl is removed by wind or traffic)	100kg of NaCl	85kg of NaCl	170kg of NaClor 85 kg of mixture
c) -4 or higher, temperature is falling d) -7 to -4, in shade e) -12 to -7 in sun	55 to 115kg of NaCl or mixture (if NaCl is removed by wind or traffic)	170 to 225kg of NaCl or 135kg of mixture	130kg of NaCl	170 to 280kg of NaClor 170kg of mixture
f) -7 to -4, temperature is falling g) -12 to -7, in shade h) -18 to -12, in sun	70 to 140kg of NaCl or mixture	165kg of mixture	170kg of mixture	280kg of mixture
-18 to -12, in sun	No chemical application	No chemical application	210kg of mixture	340kg of mixture or 1700kg of treated abrasive (abrasive mixed with salt)
Below -18	No chemical application	No chemical application	Abrasive mixed with salt	340kg of mixture or 1700kg of treated abrasive (abrasive mixed with salt)

Note 1: All mixtures in the above table are NaCl and $CaCl_2$ in a 3:1 ratio
Note 2: All quantities (above) are given in kg per km of two-lane road

---

[54] From Keyser (1981)

RELATED TECHNICAL ISSUES

Logistics in mountainous regions

In mountain areas poor accessibility can severely affect the feasibility of hauling water for use in refugee camps. Possible haulage methods include use of water trucks or tanks pulled by tractors, although difficulties can be expected with water spilling out of tanks on steep gradients. Winter weather could make access problems worse. Transport of water tanks, full of potable water, by means of helicopters was used in the mountains of Northern Iraq in 1991, although the operation was extremely expensive.

The logistics for supplying shelters, blankets, other materials and food are also, obviously, potentially very difficult. One possibility that has proved necessary in the past (e.g. to supply the Kurdish people in Northern Iraq) has been for civilian NGOs to work with the military, co-ordinating air drops and other supply routes. Although many NGOs are reluctant to work with the military, on the grounds that working with the military may compromise the neutral status of NGOs, in some circumstances military logistical expertise should not be ignored, even if only to seek logistical advice. The military have experience of using both air-drops and pack animals to transport water and materials into otherwise inaccessible areas.

Supply by air

Transporting equipment for water supply or sanitation facilities by helicopter is the only quick way to reach some mountainous areas, assuming there are no roads to the area. Helicopters have been used successfully (if expensively) to bring water, in tanks, to refugee supply points in the mountains.

In 1991, in Northern Iraq, air drops of potable water, in plastic bottles strapped to pallets, were made using C90 Hercules aircraft. Approximately 95 per cent of all bottles broke upon impact with the ground.[55] Air drops of food or materials, including those used in water and sanitation construction, may be more feasible, but airdrops are so expensive that other methods of transport should be used whenever possible. Airdrops are the option of last resort.

Use of pack animals

Use of pack animals is a common transport solution in many mountainous countries, for example in Nepal. The British army sometimes uses pack animals, instead of helicopters, to transport materials, for example when the helicopters are needed elsewhere or are too expensive to use for transporting non-essential materials.

Mules, donkeys and horses are all suitable for use in mountainous regions. They can reach areas which are inaccessible to road transport and could be used to transport materials for water supply or sanitation systems, as well as tents, blankets, food and other equipment. The approximate requirements and capabilities of different animals are shown in Table 5.4 .

---

[55] Cuny (1994)

Table 5.4. Requirements of horses, donkeys and pack ponies[56]

Food (per animal per day)	10lbs (4.5kg) of hay and 10lbs (4.5kg) oats/grain
Drinking water (per animal per day)	8 to 10 gallons (40 to 50 litres)
Maximum carrying load	Pack pony or horse: 70 to 75kg Donkey: 45kg
Average speed	3 to 4mph (4 to 6km/h)
Distance covered in one day	20 to 30km

Note 1: The above figures are approximate. They will vary depending on the size of the animals and the type of terrain to be covered.

Note 2: The above figures are for guidance only. Local advice should also be sought.

5.3 Mechanics

Vehicles, pumps and generators

Diesel and other engines are almost certain to experience running problems due to the cold, especially if it is not possible to keep vehicles indoors when not in use, or if mechanical water pumps or generators have to be left outside temporarily. Petrol engines are less prone to fuel problems and would be the only choice for extremely cold areas. A good guide is to observe whether local vehicles are run on petrol or diesel.

Many starting problems can be avoided by keeping mechanical plant indoors, especially at night, or by starting the engine periodically (for example running a vehicle engine for 10 minutes every hour or two). Use the skills of *local* mechanics who will already be adept at keeping engines running in the cold.

Problems that are likely to affect the engines of vehicles and pumps are listed, with solutions, in Table 5.5.

Diesel fuel

Diesel fuel, whether local or imported, must be suitable for use in cold weather. Additives are available in some countries that, if necessary, can be put into warm-weather diesel to prevent it from gelling. In the UK this fraction is known as the 'middle distillate flow improver'; in Iran there is an additive called 'Nesto'.[57] Note that these additives must be put into the fuel in advance, and will not remedy the problem after the fuel has gelled.

---

[56] Kohler (1999)

RELATED TECHNICAL ISSUES

Table 5.5. Mechanical problems with engines

Engine problem	Solution
Diesel gels Diesel partially solidifies when left for periods of time, undisturbed, in freezing temperatures. Engine will turn over but not fire and inspection of fuel tank reveals gelled diesel.	**Prevention** Use diesel designed for use in the cold or put additives into standard diesel. Light a fire under the fuel tank at night. *Warning: diesel is not likely to catch fire, but do not try this with petrol which is highly flammable!* **Repair** Change fuel filters (which are probably clogged); fill filter casing with warm diesel and heat diesel in the tank by building a fire underneath it.
Water freezing in cooling system Check in radiator if in doubt.	**Prevention** Use more antifreeze in the cooling system. **Repair** Warm things up slowly, do not start the engine otherwise the water pump could break. Only when everything is unfrozen start the engine and look for leaks. It may be necessary to replace pipes and gaskets and/or get the radiator repaired.
Oil too viscous Engine has difficulty turning over. Only happens in extremely cold conditions or when oil is unsuitable for use in the cold.	**Prevention** Use correct grade of oil. Light fire under the engine at night (diesel vehicles only – petrol is explosive!) **Repair** Change the engine oil for a more suitable grade. Light fire underneath the engine sump.
Engine will start but runs badly Engine too cold orIcing in carburettor (petrol engines only).	**Prevention** Increase the engine idling speed, wrap multiple layers of tin foil (insulation) around various water pipes, or hang sacking over the radiator grill (reducing its efficiency to dissipate heat).

In some countries drivers mix a small quantity of petrol (gasoline) or kerosene in with the diesel fuel. Each 10 per cent by volume of added diluent will lower the 'cloud point', the temperature at which the fuel begins to gel, by about 2°C. An absolute maximum of 50 per cent of petrol must not be exceeded, since the risks of fire and explosion increase as more petrol is used. This method is only suitable for occasional use because regular use leads to reduced power output and wear of fuel injection equipment.[58]

---

[57] Goulding (1998)
[58] Owen (ed., 1989)

Diesel fuel is very likely to gel after driving from a warm area into the mountains, where the ambient temperatures are much lower, especially at night. Diesel gelling on the first night in the field will delay activities planned for the next day.

If diesel-powered pumps are left outside, the pumping cavity should be drained at night to prevent cracking from ice formation inside.

5.4 Shelter

In emergencies the functions of shelter are to protect people from the elements, to help people to feel more secure, and to provide privacy and space for personal or group needs. Transitional settlement options must also contribute to local and regional political, social, environmental and economic security, and options should be considered part of a strategy agreed between the affected population, national and local governments, host populations and the aid sectors. Water supply and sanitation decisions are dependent on first establishing the best shelter option, in cold regions as in the tropics.

Equipment which is provided to improve personal comfort may not necessarily be used for their intended purposes, so attention should be given to the choice of equipment. Certain items may be sold by the intended beneficiaries, and other items (such as doors and door frames) may be used as fuel, instead of being used for their intended purposes.

Rehabilitation of urban shelter

In the urban case, local housing is the obvious place for refugees to live, if there is any housing to spare. Community centres, schools, churches, mosques, or sports halls may also be used, as collective centres, although in this case consideration should be given to the activities displaced by using these buildings in a different way than usual.

The role of aid agencies in providing shelter for urban disasters becomes that of fixing and repairing (floors, windows, roofs, etc.). In order to improve the weather proofing and thermal retention properties of the buildings. It may be possible to employ and co-ordinate local craftsmen to do much of this work.

When people move back into previously vacated housing, there are likely to be problems of broken or frozen water supply or sewer service pipes for the houses. Advice on defrosting metal and plastic pipes in which water has frozen solid is contained in section 3.5.

Tents

Tents, huts and other shelters may be used in rural locations where there is a scarcity of proper construction materials due to strained logistics. Temporary shelter may also be necessary while reconstruction of permanent housing takes place. The proper location of tented camps is a crucial factor in cold regions: for example, poorly drained areas should be avoided. In hilly areas a temperature inversion (when cold air sinks to the valley floor) may mean that a camp located on the lower slopes of a mountain or hill is actually in a warmer location than a camp on the valley floor itself. Several factors are relevant to the use of tents in cold regions:

RELATED TECHNICAL ISSUES

- Heavy duty, waterproof, tent material is preferable to provide protection against the cold. If the material is not sufficiently waterproof then people will tend to throw plastic sheeting over the top. This can cause the tent material to rot because the plastic restricts ventilation and prevents condensation on the inside of the tent from escaping.
- Wooden, raised floors in tents help to keep the occupants warm by avoiding the need to walk, sit or sleep on the cold ground. Giving people some form of bed also significantly increases their comfort, for the same reason.
- The heat-retaining properties of tents without an in-built ground sheet can reportedly be improved by excavating the floor down by half a metre or so. This may simply cut out draughts at floor level, increasing the comfort of people sleeping on or close to the floor. Building low mud walls inside the tent has the same effect.
- Thermal tent liners, for standard UNHCR and other tents, which greatly improve their heat retention properties, are currently being developed by Shelterproject.org.[59]

---

[59] Battilana and Corselhis (2002)

Chapter 6

Human issues

6.1 Health

If the environment is cold and fuel is scarce, people tend to congregate in small, easily heated, but poorly ventilated spaces. In that way heat is conserved and maximum use is made of warm clothes, blankets and food. This behaviour and the coldness of the air encourage specific health problems, which are discussed in this section.

Air-borne diseases

Diseases: measles, pneumonia, meningitis, whooping cough, influenza, and respiratory problems

Transmission of disease through the air is the most frequent source of health problems in cold regions.[60] Efforts should be made to reduce overcrowding, provide heating, and implement measles vaccination procedures.

Water-washed diseases

Diseases transmitted by poor washing practices include faecal-oral diseases and those passed by direct human contact. Provision of washing facilities with warm water and privacy is likely to encourage good personal hygiene. Hygiene education programmes will also help to reduce the incidence of water-washed diseases.

Faecal-oral transmission

Diseases: cholera, hepatitis, typhoid, dysentery

Faecal-orally transmitted diseases are as likely to be present in cold regions as in warm ones. Pathogenic organisms do not develop as quickly in cold weather but are likely to survive much longer. In Greenland the US army detected coliform organisms in water samples taken from sites that had been abandoned four years previously.[61]

In refugee camps in very cold areas, if open defecation has been practiced previously, the winter freeze can offer an opportunity to clean up excreta from around the camp. Solid frozen

---

[60] Buttle (1998)
[61] DiGiovanni et al. (1962)

excreta can be easily removed to a burial site. This, in turn, reduces the likelihood of outbreaks of faecal-oral disease in the spring when the excreta would have thawed.

If no hot water is available or there is no method of drying hands, people may be reluctant to wash their hands after defecating, due to the discomfort involved. Methods of providing hot water are discussed in section 3.4, and a possible hand-washing facility is shown in Figure 4.2.

Water as a method of anal cleansing may also be impractical, again for reasons of comfort. Alternative methods, for example using paper, can be proposed but may not be culturally acceptable. In that case sensitive discussion of the subject with the people and with community leaders is vital to maintain effective camp sanitation.

Transmission by direct contact

Diseases: Skin and eye diseases, scabies, conjunctivitis, trachoma, mycosis

Efforts to alleviate crowding and to keep people warm enough that they do not have to huddle together will reduce the levels of transmission of skin and eye diseases. If possible the provision of hot water will greatly encourage people, especially children, to wash themselves.

Diseases transmitted by vectors

Mosquitoes

Although mosquitoes are not able to survive in consistently cold areas, there are some countries, such as Azerbaijan, where they exist in sufficient number in the summertime for malaria to be endemic, despite having severe winters. Mosquitoes are also known to transmit diseases other than malaria.

Flies

Flies develop more slowly in cold weather and, while they could be transmitters of faecal-oral disease in warm regions, this is unlikely anywhere where the ambient temperature is less than 0°C. Measures to manage sanitation and solid waste will also minimise fly breeding.

Lice

Diseases: typhus, recurrent fever

Lice are transmitted from person to person very easily in cold regions. First, because people may huddle together and secondly because lice eggs in clothes will not be killed by cold water.

Lice are difficult to treat effectively. Possible measures include:

- powdering people and clothes;
- washing clothes in hot water, although the temperature of the water must be quite high. A temperature of 70°C for one hour is necessary, according to MSF (1994), or 54°C according to Davis and Lambert (1995);
- hot ironing of clothes, after washing them, will also help to kill lice eggs present in the seams of clothing; and
- reduction of overcrowding.

Other health problems
Other likely health problems in cold climates include:

- burns from stoves;
- carbon monoxide poisoning if people use heaters in confined spaces without adequate ventilation;
- exposure caused by low temperatures, inadequate food, shelter, blankets or clothes. See also the section below on the effects of wind-chill;
- physical injury from slipping and falling on ice or frozen ground;
- falling into water, through thin ice; and
- people getting stuck in the snow in their cars without adequate equipment.

Wind-chill
Increasing wind speeds have the effect of making the human body feel colder than the temperature recorded by thermometers. This effect is known as the wind-chill effect. It is caused by the wind increasing the rate of evaporation of water from the surface of the body, which removes heat. Figure 6.1 shows how, for different air temperatures, the apparent temperature decreases as the wind speed increases. Note that the effect would be even more pronounced if people were wet, after rain for example, which would cause the body to lose heat even more quickly.

6.2 Socio-political issues
The cold can affect attitudes and morale, especially in winter. On the other hand, people involved in emergencies in cold climatic regions may have a wealth of knowledge to draw on because they have always lived in cold countries.

Some possible negative effects of the winter on water and sanitation provision are:

- Motivation of workers (including aid workers) may be generally lower in winter than in summer.
- As winter approaches the priorities of local people will probably become food, fuel, shelter and obtaining income. Water and sanitation may not be a high priority for them at that time of year. They may be used to constructing water and sanitation facilities in the warmer months only.

More developed countries (many cold region countries are more developed) have more to lose when disaster strikes. When disaster strikes a country with highly developed infrastructure and communications systems, the resulting damage is greater, in monetary terms, than that which a less developed country would experience. People in developed countries are reliant on shops for basic commodities and may also have fewer practical survival skills than people from less developed countries.

Local political systems will greatly affect material supply. Politics, corruption and bureaucracy, the latter possibly imposed by the local people so that they are properly consulted on aid issues, can all make it difficult to procure necessary items.

HUMAN ISSUES

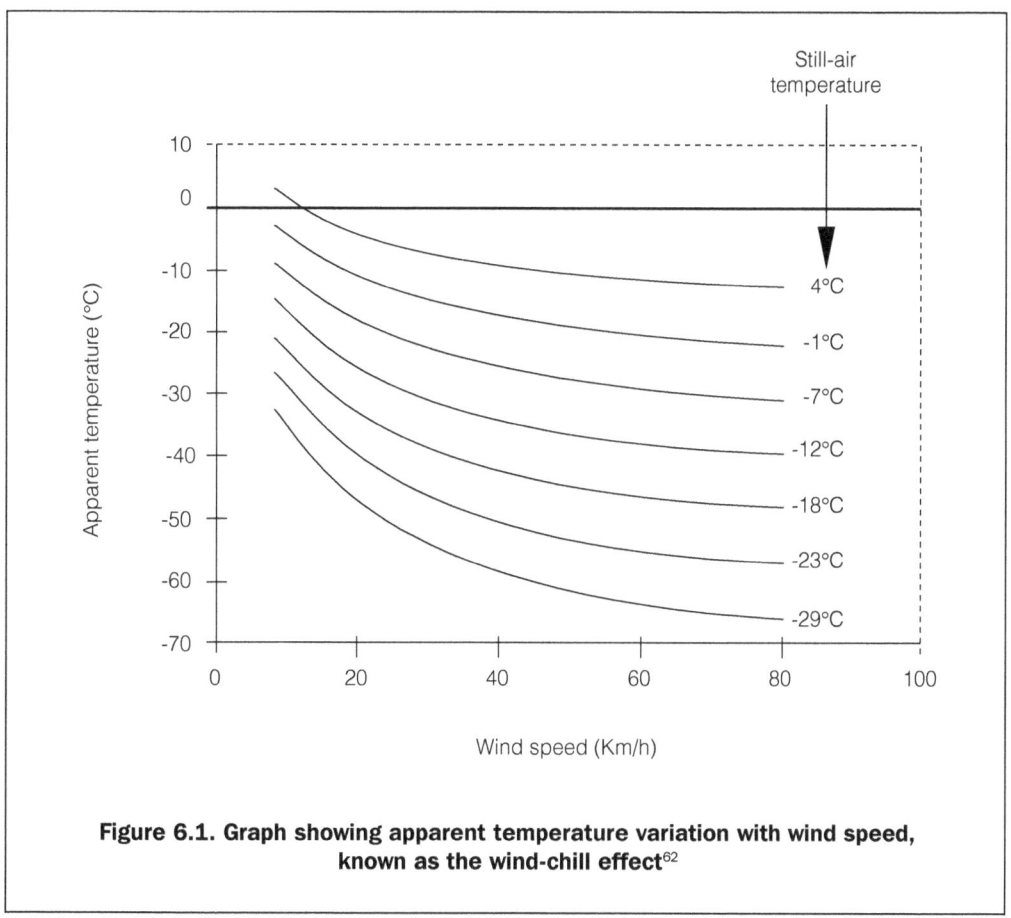

Figure 6.1. Graph showing apparent temperature variation with wind speed, known as the wind-chill effect[62]

6.3 Personal effectiveness

Warm people work more effectively, including aid workers. The value of dressing sensibly, eating properly, and consuming regular hot drinks should not be underestimated.

Some more factors that could improve the comfort and effectiveness of aid workers are:

- Personal kit should include warm, waterproof clothes, hat and gloves and sturdy boots. Note that the wind-chill factor could make conditions seem much colder than the reading on a thermometer.
- Personal medical kits should contain adequate medication for respiratory tract infections (coughs and colds).
- Ensure that vehicles have shovels, snow chains and tools as well as spare tyres. Taking food, water, and four-season sleeping bags (one per person) is also advisable.

---

[62] Figures from cdc.gov (1998)

- Beware of additional health risks such as hypothermia, frost-bite and snow-blindness. Beware also of carbon monoxide poisoning, which can be fatal and can occur when small stoves are used in badly ventilated, confined areas.
- Ensure that new staff are fully briefed about personal risks and issues relevant to working in cold regions.

6.4 Health and safety

Working in cold climates is potentially dangerous for personnel, who should adopt safe work procedures. Personnel should wear warm and protective clothing suitable for the climate and the tasks to be undertaken. Outside work should never be undertaken alone, so that assistance can be sought if one person becomes injured or gets into difficulty. Cold has a numbing effect, and people may not be immediately aware of injuries sustained.

Chapter 7

Additional information

7.1 Appendix A – Water supply flowcharts

Figures 7.1 and 7.2 can be used to consider possible water sources for emergencies in cold regions. They deal with the physical and technical aspects of water source selection alone, and should therefore be used in conjunction with Figure 7.3, which also considers the wider issues, including security, socio-political or cultural constraints, and other considerations associated with the use of each potential water source.

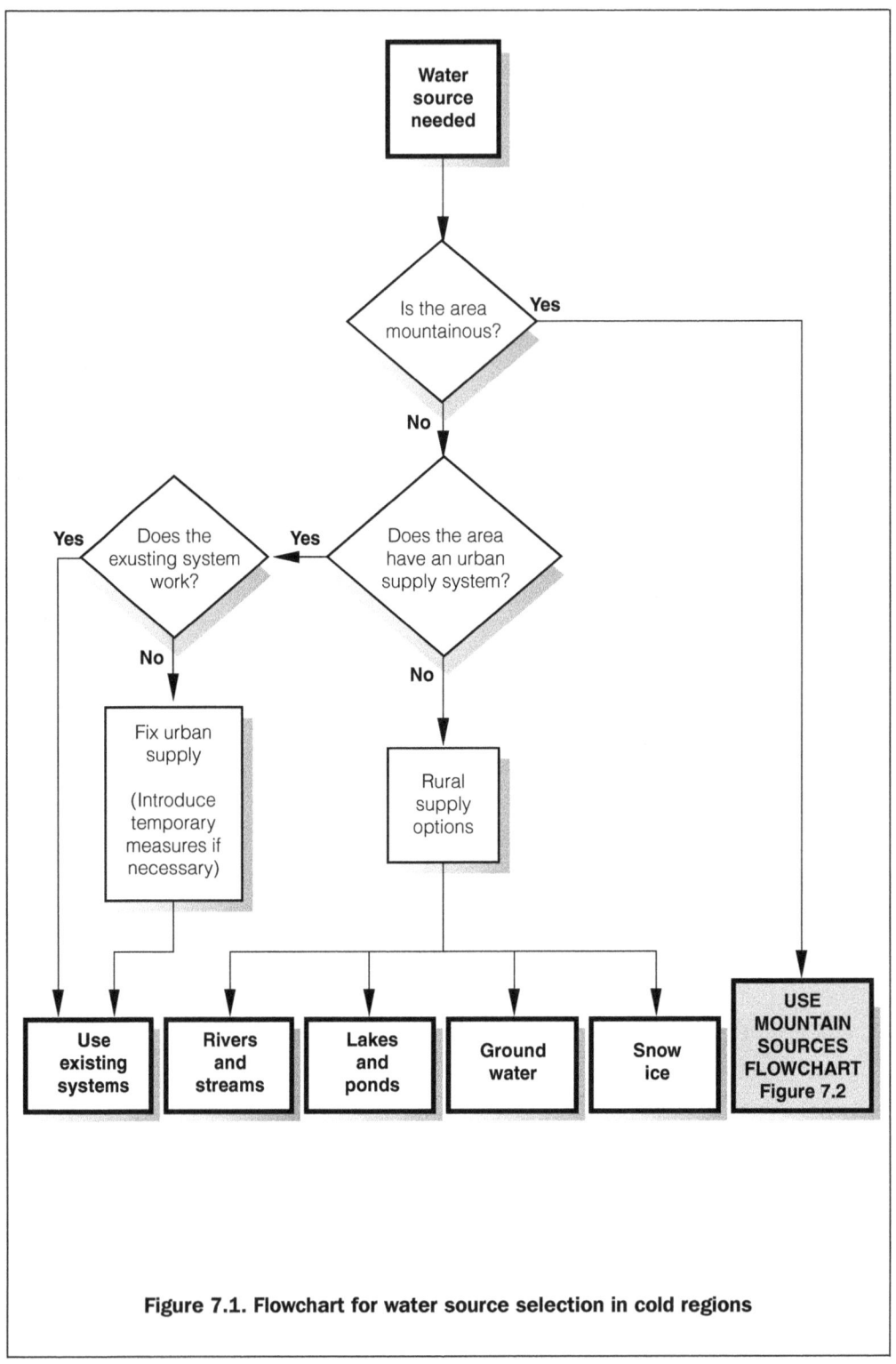

Figure 7.1. Flowchart for water source selection in cold regions

ADDITIONAL INFORMATION

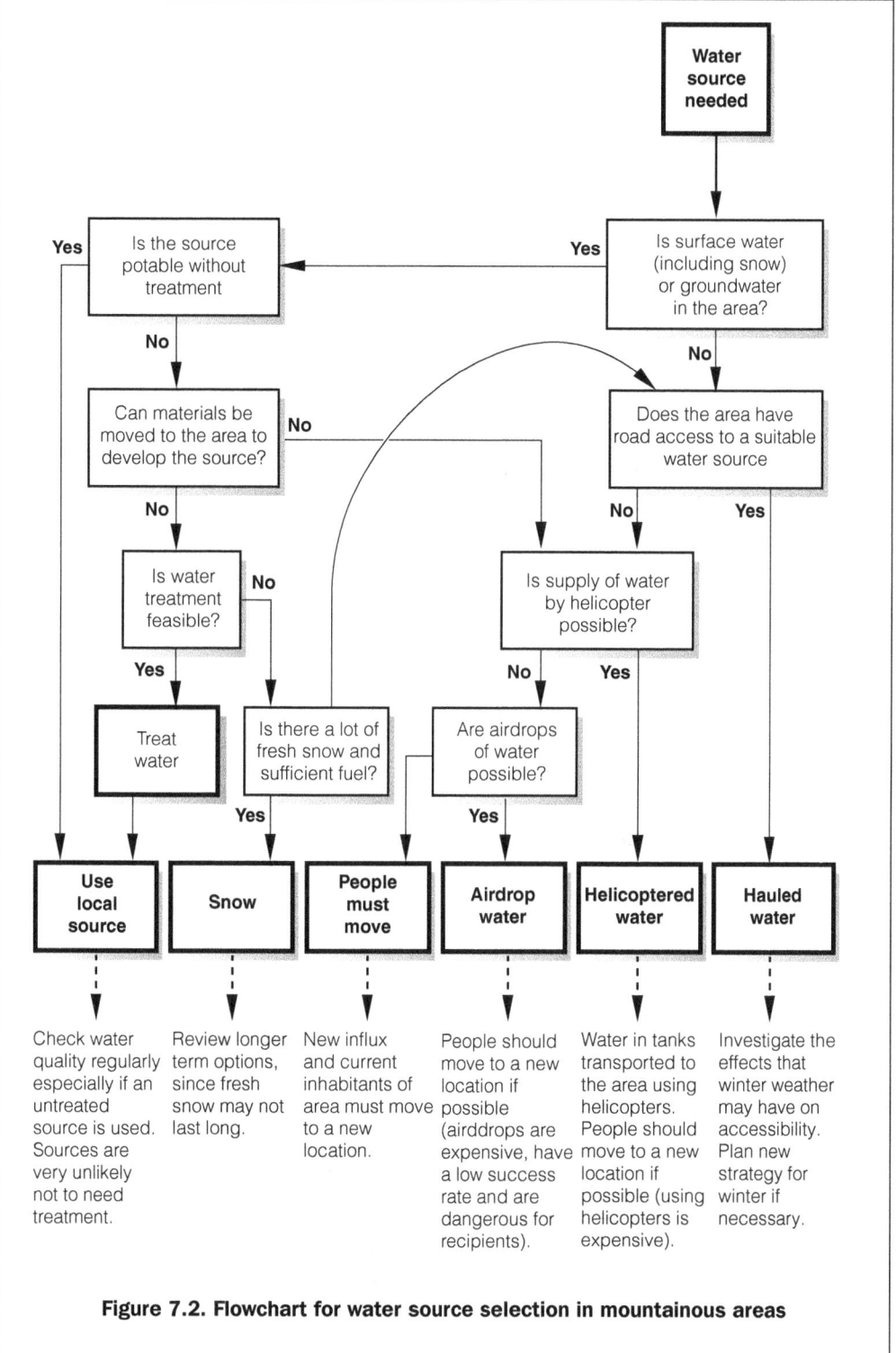

Figure 7.2. Flowchart for water source selection in mountainous areas

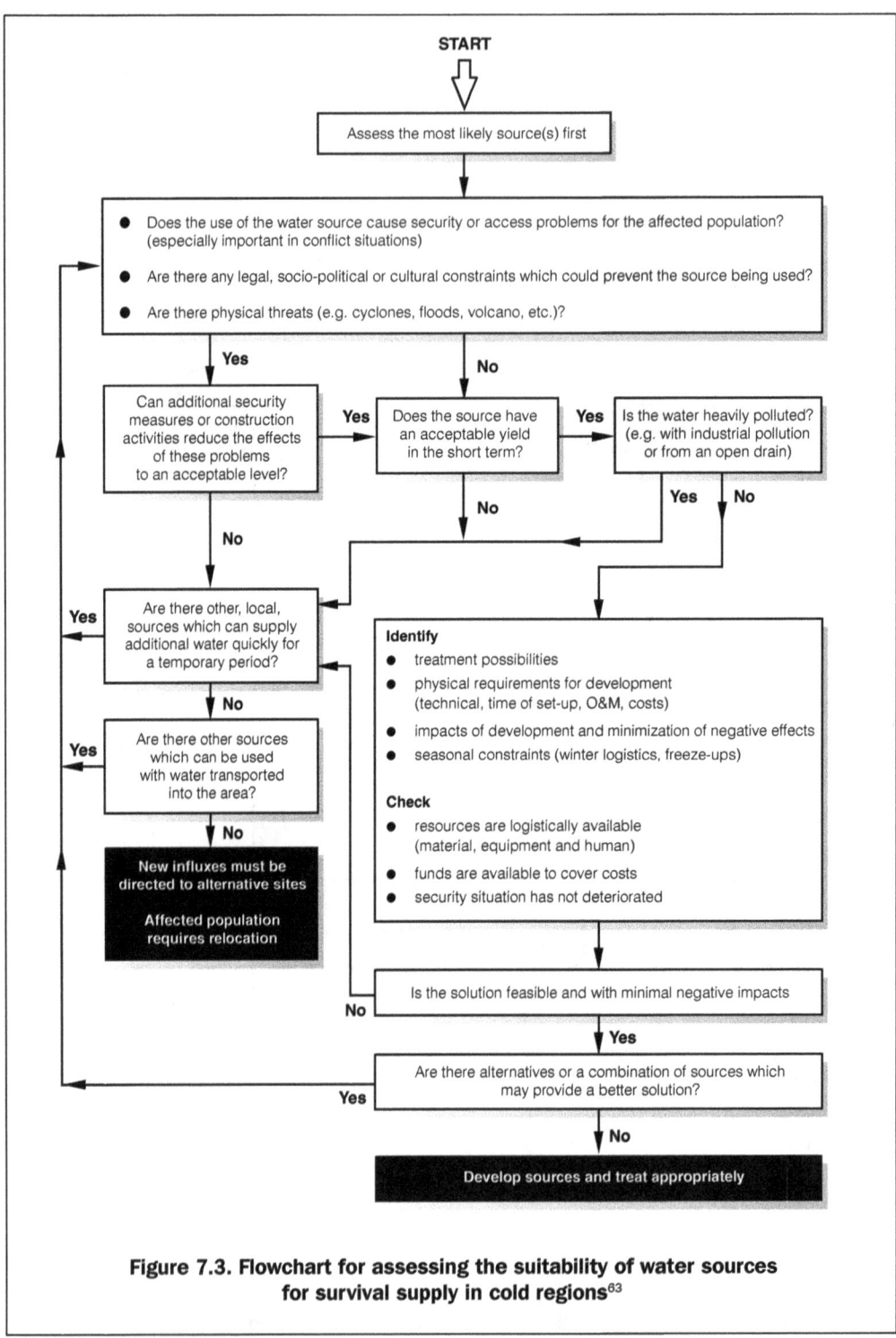

Figure 7.3. Flowchart for assessing the suitability of water sources for survival supply in cold regions[63]

---
[63] Adapted from House and Reed (1998)

ADDITIONAL INFORMATION

7.2 Appendix B – Thermal properties and density of materials

Table 7.1. Thermal properties and density of construction materials

Material	Dry density kg/m³	Specific heat capacity kJ/kg °C	Thermal conductivity W/m °C
Polyurethane foam	32	1.67	0.024
Polystyrene foam	30	1.26	0.036
Rock wool, glass wool	55	0.84	0.040
Wood, plywood, dry	600	2.72	0.17
Wood, fir or pine, dry	500	2.51	0.12
Wood, Oak, dry	700	2.09	0.17
Concrete, insulating mix	200 to 1500		0.07 to 0.60
Concrete	2000	0.67	1.7
Asphalt	2000	1.67	0.72
Wood stave			0.26
Polyethylene, high density (HDPE)	950	2.26	0.36
Polvinyl chloride, (PVC)	1400	1.05	0.19
Asbestos cement	1900		0.65
Steel	7500	0.50	43
Ductile iron	7500		50
Aluminium	2700	0.88	200
Copper	8800	0.42	375

Table 7.2. Thermal properties and density of materials found in the environment

Material	Dry density kg/m³	Specific heat capacity kJ/kg °C	Thermal conductivity W/m °C
Air, no convection (0°C)		1.00	0.024
Air film, outside, 24km/h wind (per air film)			0.86
Air film, inside (per air film)			0.24
Snow, new loose	85	2.09	0.08
Snow, on ground	300	2.09	0.23
Snow, drifted and compacted	500	2.09	0.7
Ice at -40°C	900	2.09	2.66
Ice at 0°C	900	2.09	2.21
Water at 0°C	1000	4.19	0.58
Peat, dry	250	2.09	0.07
Peat, thawed, 80% moisture	250	1.34	0.14
Peat, frozen, 80% ice	250	0.92	1.73
Peat, pressed, moist	1140	1.67	0.70
Clay, dry	1700	0.92	0.9
Clay, thawed, saturated (20%)	1700	1.76	1.6
Clay, frozen, saturated (20%)	1700	1.34	2.1
Sand, dry	2000	0.80	1.1
Sand, thawed, saturated (10%)	2000	1.21	3.2
Sand frozen, saturated (10%)	2000	0.88	4.1
Rock, typical	2500	0.84	2.2

ADDITIONAL INFORMATION

7.3 Appendix C – Surface pipes, preventing freezing [64]

Table 7.3 shows values of the 'design times', t_d, for how much time (in minutes) water in surface laid pipes will take to reach the freezing point (0°C), for different ambient temperatures and with the water starting at different initial temperatures. Design times can be used in two ways:

1. For water that has stopped flowing in a pipe, t_d is the maximum time (minutes) that the water should be allowed to stand with no risk of freezing.

2. For flowing water the maximum length of pipe, L_p, (metres), in which the water will not reach freezing temperatures can be calculated using:

$$L_p = \frac{t_d \times q_w \times 60}{A}$$

Where: L_p = Length of pipe (m)

t_d = Design time (mins)

q_w = Flow rate of water (m³/sec)

A = Internal cross sectional area of the pipe (m²)

The data in Table 7.3 can be used to make an estimate of the design time, using interpolation, or the equations which follow can be used to obtain a more accurate figure.

Notes and assumptions
1. The design time values in this section are calculated on a conservative basis. Real-life values of t_d should be slightly greater than the values given here.
2. The average wind speed has been taken as either zero (still air) or 30 km/h for these calculations. As wind speed increases the design times decrease.
3. These figures assume that heat is lost only to the air. Pipes resting on the cold ground will lose heat even more quickly than these design times. Likewise wet pipes will lose heat very quickly.
4. In the calculations pipes are assumed to be relatively thin-walled, i.e. the thickness of the pipe wall is much less than the diameter of the pipe; and the thermal resistance across the water / pipe-wall contact area is assumed to be negligible.

---

[64] Pipe products data such as wall thicknesses are taken from manufacturer's data

Table 7.3. Design times t_d for water to cool to 0°C from different starting temperatures, for surface laid pipes of different materials and diameters

Outside temp. (°C)	Design time (minutes) for zero wind speed				Design time (minutes) for wind speed = 30 km/h			
	Initial water temperature (°C)							
	1	2	5	10	1	2	5	10
50 mm (2 inch) MDPE pipe (wall thickness of 4.6 mm, pressure rating 12 bar)								
-1	189	272	377	438	84	122	171	201
-5	38	68	129	187	17	31	59	86
-10	17	33	69	110	8	15	32	51
-15	11	21	46	77	5	10	21	36
-20	8	15	34	59	4	7	16	28
90 mm (3.5 inch) MDPE pipe (wall thickness of 8.2 mm, pressure rating 10 bar)								
-1	404	583	810	945	186	270	381	452
-5	82	147	279	404	39	69	133	195
-10	38	70	149	239	18	34	72	116
-15	23	45	99	168	11	22	48	82
-20	17	32	73	128	8	16	36	63
50 mm (2 inch) PVC pipe (wall thickness of 2.5 mm, pressure rating 9 bar)								
-1	189	272	376	437	84	122	171	200
-5	38	68	129	186	17	31	59	86
-10	17	33	69	110	8	15	32	51
-15	11	21	46	77	5	10	21	36
-20	8	15	34	59	4	7	16	27
100 mm (4 inch) PVC pipe (wall thickness of 4.5mm, pressure rating 9 bar)								
-1	460	663	921	1074	210	306	432	512
-5	94	167	317	459	44	79	151	220
-10	43	80	169	272	20	38	81	132
-15	27	51	113	191	13	25	55	93
-20	19	37	83	145	9	18	41	71
118 mm (DN 100 mm) ductile iron pipe (wall thickness of 9 mm, working pressure rating 40 bar)								
-1	529	757	1039	1195	222	318	437	502
-5	106	188	354	507	44	79	149	213
-10	47	89	187	297	20	37	79	125
-15	29	56	123	207	12	24	52	87
-20	21	40	91	157	9	17	38	66
170 mm (DN 150 mm) ductile iron pipe (wall thickness of 10 mm, working pressure rating 40 bar)								
-1	834	1195	1639	1885	351	502	689	793
-5	167	296	558	799	70	125	235	336
-10	75	140	295	469	32	59	124	197
-15	46	88	195	327	19	37	82	138
-20	33	63	143	248	14	27	60	104

ADDITIONAL INFORMATION

Equations used to calculate design times[65]

Values of t_d can be calculated using the design equation:

$$t_d = \frac{A \times R \times C \times \ln\left[\frac{T_{wi} - T_a}{T_{w0} - T_a}\right]}{60}$$

Where t_d = Design time (mins)

A = Internal cross sectional area of the pipe (m²)

R = Thermal resistance of pipe (m.°C/W)

C = Specific volumetric heat capacity of water (4,190,000J/m³°C)

T_{wi} = Initial water temperature (°C)

T_a = Ambient air temperature (°C)

T_{w0} = Water freezing temperature (0°C)

Values in the design equation are derived from:

$$R = R_p + R_{af}$$

R_p = Thermal resistance of pipe material (m°C/W)

R_{af} = Thermal resistance of pipe / air interface (m°C/W)

$$R_p = \frac{r_p - r_w}{(r_p + r_w) \times \pi \times k_p}$$

---

[65] Equations from Smith (ed., 1996)

r_p = Outer radius of pipe (m)

r_w = Inner radius of pipe (m)

k_p = Thermal conductivity of pipe material (W/m°C)

$$R_{af} = \frac{1}{2 \times \pi \times r_p \times \mu_a}$$

μ_a = Convection heat transfer coefficient at pipe / air interface (W/m²°C)

$$\mu_a = N \times W \times \left(\frac{T_{wi} - T_a}{r_p}\right)^{0.25}$$

N = Constant (1.12 W/m$^{7/4}$°C$^{5/4}$)

$$W = \sqrt{0.56 \times v_a + 1}$$

v_a = Wind speed (m/s)

ADDITIONAL INFORMATION

7.4 Appendix D – Addresses

Table 7.4. Manufacturers and suppliers

Manufacturer	Address	Products/service
Evenproducts Ltd	The Oxstalls, Evesham, Worcestershire, WR11 4TS, UK Tel: (44) 1386 41212 Fax: (44) 1386 765404 Email: bob@evenproducts.com Website: www.evenproducts.com	Oxfam-type water tanks and tank roofs in PVC and galvanised steel
Stella-Meta	Laverstoke Mill, Whitchurch, Hants., RG28 7NR, UK Tel: (44) 1256 895959 Fax: (44) 1256 892074 Email: marketing@pcimem.com Website: www.stella-meta.com	Portable water treatment units (British army supplier)
SDL Technologies	4 Habosem St., PO Box 6699, Ashdod 77166, Israel Tel: (972) 8 856 4314 Fax: (972) 8 852 4289 Email: sdl@netvision.net.il Website: www.sdl-tech.com	Portable water treatment units (Israeli) 5 to 200m^3/hr container units
Clearwater PLC	Clearwater House, Clearwater Industrial Park, Bristol Road, Bridgewater, Somerset, TA6 4AW, UK Tel: (44) 990 275252 Fax: (44) 1498 880285	Wastewater treatment (RBC) units
Klargester Environmental Ltd	College Road, Aston Clinton, Aylesbury, Bucks., HP22 5EW, UK Tel: (44) 1296 633 000 Fax: (44) 1296 631 770 Email: sales@klargester.co.uk Website: www.klargester.co.uk	RBC units, also portable version in container units
Urecon Ltd	1800 Ave. Bedard, St. Lazare-de-Vaudreuil, Quebec, J7T 2G4, Canada Tel: (1) 450 455 0961 Fax: (1) 450 455 0350 Email: urecon@urecon.com Website: www.urecon.com	Pre-insulated HDPE pipes

Table 7.5. Agencies and organisations

Name	Address	Function or service
REDR	1 Great George Street, London, UK Tel: (44) 20 7233 3116 Fax: (44) 20 7222 0564 Website: www.redr.org	Register of engineers available for disaster relief work
UNHCR	Centre William Rappard, 154 Rue de Lausanne, 1202 Geneva 21, Switzerland Tel: (41) 22 739 8111 Fax: (41) 22 731 9546 Website: www.unchr.ch	UN commission concerned with the well-being of refugees. Often acts as a co-ordinating organisation in the field.
IFRC	17 Chemin des Crets, PO Box 372, 1211 Geneva 19, Switzerland Tel: (41) 22 730 4222 Fax: (41) 22 730 0395 Website: www.ifrc.org	International Federation of Red Cross and Crescent Societies International humanitarian organisation
ICRC	19 Avenue de la Paix, CH 1202, Geneva, Switzerland Tel: (41) 22 734 6001 Fax: (41) 22 733 2057 Website: www.icrc.org	International humanitarian/aid organisation
MSF France	8 Rue Saint-Sabin, 75544 Paris Cedex 11, France Tel: (33) 1 40 21 29 29 Fax: (33) 1 48 06 68 68 Website: www.msf.org	International aid organisation
Oxfam (GB)	274 Banbury Road, Oxford, OX2 7DZ, UK Tel: (44) 1865 311 311 Fax: (44) 1865 312 600 Website: oxfam.org.uk	International aid and development organisation
Shelter project.org	Website: www.shelterproject.org	Emergency shelter research group

7.5 References and bibliography

Alter, Amos J and Cohen, Jules B, 1969, *Cold Region Water Storage Practices*, in *Public Works* (USA), (1969), Vol. 100, Part 10

Andregg, J A, Hubbs, G L and Eaton, E R, (1960), 'Ice Water on Tap for the Arctic', in *Water Works Engineering*, July 1960

Assar, M, (1971), *Guide to Sanitation in Natural Disasters*. WHO, Geneva, Switzerland

Battilana, Rachel and Corsellis, Tom, (2002), *Personal Communication*, Shelterproject.org

Boyd, D W, Schriever, W R and Taylor, D A, (1981), 'Snow and Buildings' in Gray, D M and Male, D H (ed), 1981, *Handbook Of Snow, Principles, Processes, Management and Use*, Pergamon Press, Willowdale, Ontario, Canada

Buttle, Mark A, (1998), *Out in the Cold, Emergency Water Supply and Sanitation for Cold Regions*. MSc Dissertation, Water Engineering and Development Centre (WEDC), Loughborough, UK

Cairncross, S and Feacham, R, (1993), *Environmental Health Engineering in the Tropics*, Second Edition. Wiley, Chichester, UK

Carter, W Nick, (1991), *Disaster Management, A Disaster Manager's Handbook*. Asian Development Bank, Manila, Phillippines

Chalinder, Andrew, (1994), 'Water and Sanitation in Emergencies, Good Practice Review No. 1', *Relief and Rehabilitation Network*, ODI, London, UK

Crites, Ronald W, and Tchobanoglous, George, (1998), *Small and Decentralized Wastewater Management Systems*, McGraw-Hill, NY, USA.

Cuny, Frederick C, (1994), *An Assessment of Airdrops in Relief Operations*. Intertect, Dallas, Texas, USA

Davis, Jan and Lambert, Robert, (1995), *Engineering in Emergencies, A Practical Guide for Relief Workers*. IT Publications, London, UK

DiGiovanni, C, Rachlin, J W, Barquist, R F, Dooley, E S and David, T R A, (1962), 'Some Microbiological and Sanitary Aspects of Military Operations in Greenland', in *Arctic* Vol. 15, USA

Easson, M Elaine, Dicp, Tam M, Hargrave, Gregory A, Dean, Mary and McGarry, Michael G, (1988), 'Sanitation Technologies for Temperate and Cold Climates', *Environmental Sanitation Review No. 25*, August (1988), Environmental Sanitation Information Centre, Asian Institute of Technology, Bangkok, Thailand

Franceys, R, Pickford, J and Reed, R, (1992), *A Guide to the Development of On-site Sanitation*. World Health Organisation, Geneva

Gould, Toby, 2001, 'Simple measures make all the difference', in *Waterlines* Vol. 19, No. 3, January 2001

Goulding, Bruce, 1998, personal communication, Training Co-ordinator, Exodus Expeditions, London, UK

Gros, William F H, 1980, 'Leak-Detection Problems in Cold Weather Conditions', in *Distribution Systems – Actions and Innovations*. American Water Works Association (AWWA)

Harvey, P, Baghri, S and Reed, R, (2002), *Emergency Sanitation*.

Hendricks, David, (ed.), (1991), *Manual of Design for Slow Sand Filtration*, American Water Works Association (AWWA) Research Foundation, Denver, Colorado, USA

House, Sarah and Reed, Bob, (1997), *Emergency Water Sources, Guidelines for Selection and Treatment*, WEDC, Loughborough, UK

Huisman, L and Wood, W E, (1974), *Slow Sand Filtration*. World Health Organisation (WHO), Geneva, Switzerland

ITeM, (1995), *The World (1995/96), A Third World Guide*. Instituto del Tercer Mundo, Mosca Hnos, Uruguay

Jordan, Thomas D, (1984), *A Handbook of Gravity-flow Water Systems (for Small Communities)*. IT Publications, London, UK

Keyser, J Hode, (1981), 'Chemicals and Abrasives for Snow and Ice Control', in Gray, D M and Male, D H, *Handbook of Snow: Principles, Processes. Management and Use*. Pergamon Press, Ontario, Canada

Kohler, M H K, (1999), personal communication, British Army Pack Animal Centre, UK

Krylov, Boris A, 1998, Cold Weather Concreting,, CRC Press, Boca Raton, USA

Langham, E J, (1981), 'Physics and Properties of Snowcover', in Gray, D M and Male, D H, *Handbook of Snow: Principles, Processes. Management and Use*. Pergamon Press, Ontario, Canada

Larson, Lloyd A, (1976), 'Cold Weather Operation of Elevated Storage Tanks', in the *American Water Works Association Journal*, Vol. 68, Part 10

Marino, Lynn, (1997), 'Alaskan Water and Sewer Systems: Confusion and Challenges in the Rural Arctic', in *Water Nepal*. Vol. 5 No. 2, Jul-Dec 1997

Mears, Catherine and Chowdhury, Sue, (1994), *Health Care for Refugees and Displaced People. Oxfam Practical Health Guide No. 9*. Oxfam, Oxford, UK

Metcalf and Eddy, (1991), *Wastewater Engineering: Treatment, Disposal and Reuse*. 3rd Edition, revised by George Tchobanoglous and Franklin Burton, Series in Water Resources and Environmental Engineering. McGraw-Hill Inc., New York, NY, USA.

MSF, 1994, *Public Health Engineering in Emergency Situations*. MSF, Paris, France

Nelson, LaVern M, (1980), 'Frozen Water Services', in *Distribution Systems – Actions and Innovations*. American Water Works Association (AWWA).

Ockwell, Ron, (1986), *Assisting in Emergencies, A Resource Handbook for UNICEF Field Staff*. UNICEF, Geneva, Switzerland

Owen, K (ed.), (1989), 'Gasoline and Fuel Additives', *Critical Reports on Applied Chemistry*. Volume 25. Society of Chemical Industry (SCI), Wiley, Chichester, UK.

Patwardhan, A D, (1989), *Chlorination and the use of Chlorinators*. Indian Water Works Association, Bombay, India

Pearce, E A and Smith, C G, (1998), World Weather Guide, Helicon, Oxford, UK

Perrin, Pierre, (1996), *Handbook on War and Public Health*. ICRC, Geneva, Switzerland

Potts, Eddie, (1991), 'The Mobile Support Team in Northern Iraq', Workshop No. 2 Discussion Paper, in Reed (ed.), *Technical Support for Refugees*, WEDC, Loughborough, UK

Rajagopalan, S and Shiffman, M A, (1974), *Guide to Simple Sanitary Measures for the Control of Enteric Diseases*. WHO, Geneva, Switzerland

RedR, (1986), *Outline Approach to Disaster Relief*, First Edition, RedR, London, UK

Reed, Bob (ed.), (1991), *Technical Support for Refugees*, WEDC, Loughborough, UK

Reinbold, Frederik, 2000, personal communication, Technical Team Leader, Oxfam (GB) in Kosovo, 1999

Ryan, William L, (1990), 'Surface Water Supplies', in Ryan William L and Crissman, Randy D, *Cold Region Hydrology and Hydraulics*, Technical Council on Cold Regions Engineering Monograph, ASCE, New York, NY, USA

SCF, (1994), *Health Care in Shelters in Emergencies*. SCF, London, UK

Smith, D W (ed.,) (1996), *Cold Regions Utilities Monograph*. Third Edition, ASCE, New York, NY, USA

ADDITIONAL INFORMATION

Smith, M D, (1999), *Water and Environmental Health*. Distance Learning Module, WEDC, Loughborough, UK

Steppuhn, H, (1981), 'Snow and Agriculture', in Gray, D M and Male, D H, *Handbook of Snow: Principles, Processes. Management and Use*. Pergamon Press, Ontario, Canada

Swenson, Richard H and Rahe, Terrance M, 1991, 'Water and Sanitation Efforts Among Displaced Kurdish Civilians', Field Report 339, *Water and Sanitation for Health*, US Agency for International Development, Washington DC

UNHCR, (1982), *Handbook for Emergencies, Part One, Field Operations*. UNHCR, Geneva, Switzerland

UNHCR, (1992), Water *Manual for Refugee Situations*, UNHCR, Programme and Technical Support Section, Geneva, Switzerland

USEPA, (1990), *Technologies for Upgrading Existing or Designing New Drinking Water Facilities*. United States Environmental Protection Agency, Washington, USA

Walker, Kevin, (1988), *Mountain Hazards*. Constable, London UK.

Internet source

US Army (1987) *Arctic and Subarctic Construction: Utilities*. (US Army Publication Number: Army TM 5-852-5/AFM 88-19, Vol 5).
<http://www.usace.army.mil/publications/armytm/tm5-852-5/>
Accessed on 25 October 2004

Index

acrylonitrile butadiene styrene 35
activated sludge 49
aid provision 3, 59
air-drops 63
anaerobic sludge digestion 49
antifreeze admixtures 56
asbestos cement 35, 77

boiling water 28, 40
boreholes 10, 12, 39, 58
break-pressure tanks 42
brine pumping 17

chemical disinfection 26
climate 2–7, 44–5, 59, 70–2
cold region, definition of 4
concrete 23–4, 27, 39, 45, 48, 55–60

defrosting pipes 35
density of materials 77–8
diesel 21, 59, 64–6
disease 6, 14, 28–9, 39, 44, 68–9
disposal of the dead 53
distribution points 5, 31, 38–9

engines 64
excreta disposal 7, 14, 44, 47, 49, 53

filtration 26–7
frost jacking 58
frozen ground 45–6, 52–3, 56–8, 70

glacial flour 27
ground storage lakes 24
groundwater 5, 10, 12, 15, 24

hand-washing 47–9
handpumps 12, 38
hauled water 6, 21
HDPE pipes 33–5, 77, 83
health problems 6, 10, 14, 39, 68, 70
honey-bags 47, 53
hot water 29, 35, 37, 47, 69
human issues 6, 68

ice control 60
ice cutting 17
infiltration galleries 17–19, 21
insulation 12, 23, 30, 33–5, 39, 55–6, 64
intakes 17–19

latrines 5–7, 44–8, 53–4
latrine slabs 45–7, 55–6
levels of development 4
lice 29, 69
logistics 2, 3, 6, 21, 40, 59, 63, 66

material properties 34
mechanics 64

open defecation 44, 54, 68

pack animals 63
percolating filters 49
personal effectiveness 71
pipe burial 33
pipe materials 33–5
polyvinylchloride 33
ponds 15, 17, 60
portable aerobic units 51
properties of snow 9
pumping 9, 12, 14, 17, 25, 37, 42, 48, 66
pumps 9, 10, 12, 14, 30, 42–3, 59, 64, 66

rivers 10, 14, 15, 17
rotating biological contactors 49, 51
roughing filtration 27

sanitation 2–8, 44, 53–4, 59, 63, 66, 69–70
sedimentation tanks 9, 26
septic tanks 51
sewerage systems 14, 48
shelter 5–6, 8, 38, 47, 55, 66
slow sand filters 26
snow loads 24
solid waste 6, 53, 54
spring protection 12
standpipes 39
storage tanks 6, 10, 21, 23, 30, 39, 57

INDEX

streams 14–15, 17, 19, 39, 60
surface laid pipes 79–80
surface water 10, 12, 14–15, 19, 39, 54

tap box 39, 41
tents 63, 66, 67
thermal properties 34–5, 77–8

vehicles 64
viscosity 7, 9, 24, 25, 26, 27

wastewater treatment 47–51
water
  density 8
  distribution 38, 39
  intakes 19
  quality 9, 14, 15, 27
  sources 9–10, 15, 21, 39–40, 60, 73, 76
  supply 2, 6–8, 39, 66, 73
  treatment 7, 10, 15, 19, 25, 40, 59, 83
wells 10
wind-chill 70
winterisation studies 5

Also available in this series:

Emergency Sanitation
Assessment and programme design

Peter Harvey, Sohrab Baghri and Bob Reed

This book is designed to assist those involved in planning and implementing emergency sanitation programmes. The main focus of the book is a systematic and structured approach to assessment and programme design. It provides a balance between the hardware (technical) and software (socio-cultural, institutional) aspects of sanitation programmes, and links short-term emergency response to long-term sustainability. The book is relevant to a wide range of emergency situations, including both natural and conflict-induced disasters, and open and closed settings. It is suitable for field technicians, engineers and hygiene promoters, as well as staff at agency headquarters. Included free with each book is a mini CD and an 'aide-memoire' to the process of planning and implementation.

384pp. (250/176)   **ISBN:** 1 84380 005 5
http://www.lboro.ac.uk/wedc/publications/es.htm

Emergency Vector Control Using Chemicals

Christophe Lacarin and Bob Reed

The control of vectors that transmit diseases in emergencies is critical to the prevention of epidemics. This handbook describes how such vectors can be identified and controlled using chemicals. Aimed at non-specialists such as logisticians, engineers and health workers, it provides advice on identifying the responsible vector, selecting the appropriate control chemical and the means of application, together with advice on planning an implementation programme.

134pp. (250/176)   **ISBN:** 0 906055 65 2
http://www.lboro.ac.uk/wedc/publications/evc.htm

Emergency Water Sources
Guidelines for selection and treatment

Sarah House and Bob Reed

These guidelines have been designed to help those involved in the assessment of emergency water sources to collect relevant information in a systematic way, to use this information to select a source or sources and to determine the appropriate level of treatment required to make the water suitable for drinking. The book is relevant to a wide range of emergency situations, including both natural and conflict-induced disasters.

320pp. (250/176)   **ISBN:** 0 906055 71 7 (second edition)
http://www.lboro.ac.uk/wedc/publications/ews.htm

www.ingramcontent.com/pod-product-compliance
Lightning Source LLC
Chambersburg PA
CBHW080253030426
42334CB00023BA/2805